My Kids Know More Than Me!

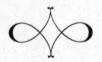

My Kids Know More Than Me!

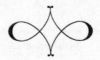

15 LIFE LESSONS
FROM Foster AND
Adopted Children

RENEE HETTICH, LMSW

ROBERT'S FAMILY
PUBLISHING

My Kids Know More than Me!

15 Life Lessons from Foster and Adopted Children

Renee Hettich, LMSW

ISBN: 978-1-942545-77-4

Library of Congress Control Number: 2016960599

Published by Robert's Family Publishing
An Imprint of Wyatt-MacKenzie

ROBERT'S FAMILY
PUBLISHING

Dedication

To my children,
Rose,
Pearl,
Marco
and
Wu LeBin
for teaching me
life's most
important lessons.

PHOTO: Moments after Renee, Rose, Pearl and Marco met Wu LeBin
in a Chinese government office, January 2015.

Foreword

WRITTEN BY

Rose Hettich, *Renee's Elder Daughter*

I'm writing this foreword to you because I want you to know what it's like to be an adopted daughter of the woman who wrote this book, and my reaction to her writing about how I've impacted her life. My mom is one of the strongest people I've gotten to know and love. She has known me the longest—for all fifteen years of my life in America. Throughout these fifteen years I've learned so much from her. I've grown up to be a very successful sixteen-year-old, and she's the one to thank.

Today, I am a junior at the local high school and I'm taking my fifth year of Spanish, one of my favorite subjects. I just got my first job as a waitress at a senior citizens home. This will allow me to pay for a school-sponsored trip abroad in the spring. I'm also proud to share that I have three younger siblings, all internationally adopted, and I love every single one of them. None of these things would be happening now for me if it weren't for my mom.

Because of how my mom has raised me, she has given me the freedom to choose who I want to be and who I will be. She has accepted my expression of who I love, what I believe in, and how I present myself to others. This is one of the greatest gifts a mother could give her daughter: opportunity for individuality.

It's more common to view the parents as the teachers in a parent-child relationship, but it's actually a mutual education. As I learn from my mom, she learns from me. This book is about what she learns from her children, but as she learns from us she is also

i

reflecting these values to us, making sure we retain them as we mature. That's what I find important in our relationship.

As the eldest child in the household, I've observed and admired the extremely passionate advocacy my mom has for children. She's always determined and persistent when it comes to standing up for her children. She passionately battles for the maximum amount of opportunities for her kids, and that is because she knows what is most important. Even before she adopted me, she was raising money for children's education and fostering emotionally (and sometimes physically) damaged children by standing up for their needs. After that, she took up the career that she has now: an adoption social worker, helping other kids find loving homes from all over the world. I like to believe that when my mom was a child, she somehow already knew that she was going to become some kind of hero who would save hundreds, if not thousands, of kids. I'm extremely lucky to be one of them. My mom is very modest about her role as my only parent, so of course, she'd say that she was the lucky one to have me as her daughter.

When my mother fought for my education, she knew of my potential. She refused for it to go to waste. Because of her passion to make sure her kids' needs are always well met, she meets with people in the educational system to discuss changes the educators and/or nurses can do to make learning easier for each child. She *always* insists that the child being discussed is present, because she knows that we know ourselves the best. We know what we need to be successful. For every child she has taken under her wing, she has fought a ferocious battle. Her passion for children inspires me to fight for what I'm passionate for.

I'm a very empathetic person, sometimes to the extremes. I constantly put my tiny feet into everyone's shoes, occasionally without their permission. Perhaps it's because of how my mom raised me. She is always trying to see things the way we do. She wants to understand us and know why we do things the way we do them and how we perceive things. I find it exceptionally interesting, and I'm very grateful. If she didn't try to see my side of the story, there would be a lot more arguments, problems, and lack of communication between us. I don't think we would have the amount of trust in each other that we have now, either. My mom also helps us by seeing what we see because she realizes that we're not perfect, and we need things in order to find success like finally hitting a yellow ball pitched during a baseball game or getting on a travel team for softball.

My mom told me once that every child is a puzzle, and as each new piece gets added, it helps to reveal a beautiful picture in the end. So in learning more about your child, whether it is that they love all things with wheels, or try to do every sport known to man, or they have an insatiable craving for chips, or they communicate through multiple languages, you put one more piece of the puzzle together. With every puzzle piece, you build new connections, and you get closer to understanding your child. You'll never finish the puzzle; there will always be things about your child you may never fully understand, but that's the fun part. There are always new pieces to discover, as people are constantly changing. It's the journey, not the destination. Each child is one of a kind and has a different picture to be discovered. Each piece to every child is unique and personal, and being able to learn about these pieces of their life is a privilege and a gift.

Throughout my mother's journey in caring for children temporarily and permanently, she has changed so many lives—including hers and mine. I couldn't be more proud to be adopted by such a special woman in this fascinating world of ours. Hopefully after reading this book, you'll realize how important foster-parenting and adopting is to the world. You'll realize how parenting can change your life, and how taking a child under your wing will change the world through their hands that have been guided by yours. Enjoy the journey, and embrace each lesson that my mom has learned through raising eight foster children and four internationally adopted children.

Rose Hettich
Renee's first adopted daughter, 16 years old, 2016

Acknowledgements

Renee wishes to thank her parents, Robert and Donna Hettich, for their guidance and encouragement and for being exceptional parents from whom she learned how to parent her children. She is grateful to her siblings for their endless support. Renee is very glad to have had her parents, sisters (Doreen and Denise), and her Aunt Nila join her on the journeys to China and Guatemala to adopt her children. She also wants to thank her children's teachers, coaches, medical specialists, and adoption social workers for their insight into and their treatment of her children's unique needs. Most important, she wishes to thank her children (foster and adopted) for teaching her the most important lessons in life.

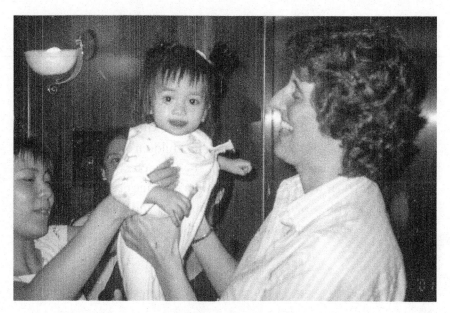

PHOTO: The very first moment as a family. Rose being given to her mom in a hotel in China, May 2001.

Table of Contents

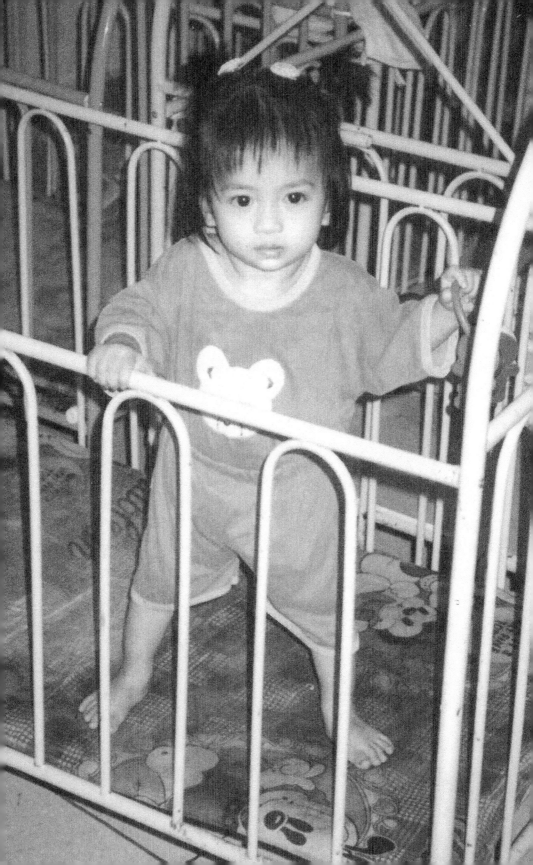

Rose

PHOTO ABOVE: Rose at 16 years old, a few days after she donated 14 inches of her beautiful
black hair to an organization that makes wigs for children with cancer.

PHOTO LEFT: Rose standing in her crib in her orphanage in southern China just a month
before she became Renee's daughter.

Pearl

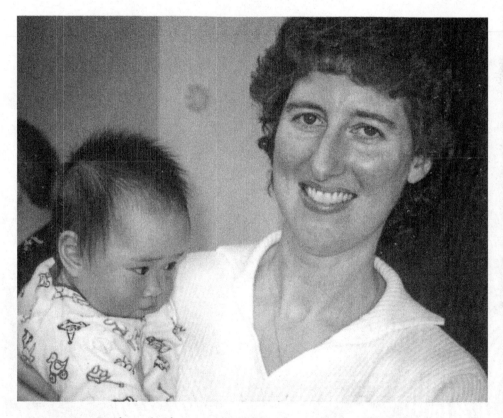

PHOTO ABOVE: Pearl meeting her mom in a Chinese government office at 9 months of age.

PHOTO RIGHT: Pearl playing shortstop for a competitive softball team, summer 2016.

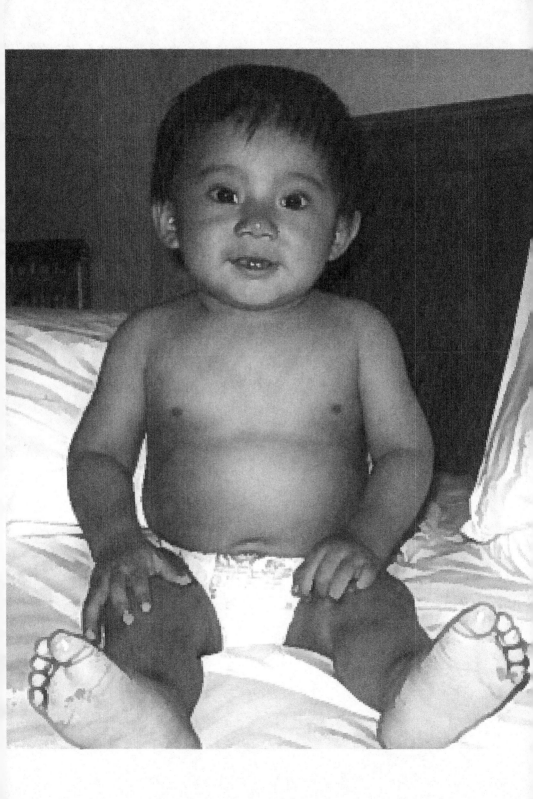

Marco

PHOTO ABOVE: Marco wading in a local creek near our home, summer 2016.

PHOTO LEFT: Marco relaxing in a Guatemalan hotel a few days after his adoption, April 2007.

Wu Le Bin

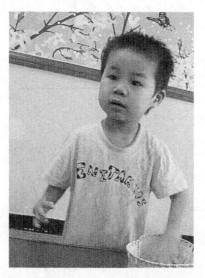

PHOTO ABOVE: The first picture of Wu LeBin provided to Renee.
He is 6.5 years old playing in his orphanage.

PHOTO ABOVE: Wu LeBin with his mom at the Guangzhou Zoo
a week after his adoption, January 2015.

PHOTO ABOVE: Wu LeBin's very special relationship with JoJo, the family cat.

An Introduction

I'm learning more from my children than they will ever learn from me. Over the past twenty-five years, I have parented twelve children through foster care and adoption. In addition, since 2005, I have been a social worker in the field of adoption, supporting hundreds of families who have adopted children of all ages and abilities from the United States and abroad. I cared for four foster families with eight children over a period of five years. All the children (and parents) arrived with emotional and behavioral challenges that were humbling. I hope each child and parent left my care stronger and better prepared for the potential of a successful future. I certainty grew with every foster care experience and learned many valuable lessons. For the past fifteen years, I have been parenting my children who joined my family through inter-country adoption. My daughters came home from China as infants, my older son arrived as a baby from Guatemala, and my younger son lived in a Chinese orphanage for disabled children until he joined our family just before his eighth birthday. All of my children are unique and special. All of my children have altered the course of my life and have brought a new understanding of the world and new clarity to what is important in life.

Most parents, when asked what they have learned from their kids, say with a smirk "patience." I hope that I have been patient with my children, at least most of the time. However, my children did not teach me patience; they demanded it. What they are teaching me is much more important. I am learning resiliency, compassion, playfulness, persistence, forgiveness, trust, responsiveness, and gratefulness from my children. They are teaching me how to listen, how to look at life through their eyes, and how to trust their expertise. My kids have prepared me to expect the unexpected (and be okay with that) and to attend to what is important and dismiss the trivial. I have learned that my children's birth families are an integral and important part of our family forever. My children have also shown me how to live my life with purpose.

This book shares true stories of how foster and adopted children teach us important lessons and inspire new understandings. This book contains stories of experiences with my foster and adopted children and how they shaped my life and worldview. Each chapter (with the exception of Four Days in China) is organized in the same manner: first I introduce the lesson I have learned from my children, then I illustrate the lesson with two to five stories about my and my children's experiences, and then I share a conclusion regarding what my children have taught me through their stories.

I have written the stories directly to my children. Some of the stories are short and sweet and others are long and complex, but each is poignant in its own way. Each story has many lessons, but they are featured in the chapter that demonstrates their most important lesson. My foster children's names have been changed and their stories have been altered slightly to protect each child's identity. My adopted children have given me permission to write their stories and use their names. They have read and agreed with the content and intent of each story.

Four Days In China

15 LESSONS

Rose, adopted in 2001 at 11 months of age

After a year and a half of tortuous waiting, I was finally traveling to China to adopt you, my first forever daughter. I was scheduled to leave in a month and travel with two other families who I was getting to know by e-mail and phone. Then very unexpectedly, I received a call from my adoption agency stating that I could travel two weeks earlier with families from another adoption agency. There would be eleven families that I wouldn't know, and I would only have two weeks to prepare to leave. The adoption agency offered this expedited travel to only my family. I was very grateful and I am still in wonder of how this one seemingly insignificant gesture changed (saved) our future. I have to admit that I debated this choice. Could we get ready that quickly? Did we want to travel in such a big group of families? How would we feel traveling with families that we didn't know? But of course, I couldn't wait to hold you in my arms. You were what was important. So your aunt, your grandparents, and I packed quickly, expedited our visas, and boarded the plane two weeks early.

Seven months before we got on the plane, before I even knew you, I had a dream about you waiting for me in a Chinese orphanage. I wrote in my journal, *"I had a dream about you last night. I remember holding onto you really tight and worrying that something was wrong. I can't wait for you to be in my arms instead of in my dreams."* I know now that at the time of this dream you were four months old and living in a rural and impoverished orphanage in southern China.

3

It was impossible for me to know at the time that something would be terribly wrong; that you would be very ill when placed in my arms in China. That your life would be in peril.

Your grandparents, your aunt, and I boarded one of the many planes we would take to get to China. It would take us four different planes and twenty-four hours to arrive in China. Our longest flight would be fourteen hours from Detroit to Beijing. Of course, I was so excited to meet you that I couldn't sleep on that very long and crowded flight. During the flight I kept saying over and over to myself, "Please let her be healthy. I can handle anything but please, please let her be well."

It was 7:30 in the evening on May 27, 2001, when your grandparents, aunt, and I were anxiously waiting for your arrival in our hotel room in Nanning, China. Shortly after that, we heard, "The babies are here!" All the families rushed to the elevators to greet their new daughters. You were the last child to get off the elevator. I recognized you immediately with your big beautiful eyes and long hair in pig tails standing straight up on the top of your head. You were also wearing one of the outfits I sent to your Social Welfare Institute (orphanage) in a care package before I traveled to adopt you. Your caregiver recognized me and waved at me to come over to meet you. In the care package I had sent to your orphanage, I included a photo album with pictures of me and your extended family so your caregiver knew who I was. You were very quiet and looked at me cautiously. I touched your arm and said nǐ hǎo (hello). The adoption facilitator, Shelly, took you from your caregiver and placed you into my arms. You were so tiny. The outfit that you were wearing was a size 0-3 months, even though you were eleven months old. It was a little short, but otherwise it fit. You did not seem frightened. You did not cry and you did not show any interest in returning to your caregiver like many of the other babies did.

After we took a few pictures of you with your grandparents, and aunt, and me in front of the elevators, we returned to our hotel room for our first few moments as a family. You were so quiet. You just looked at me with your deep black eyes. You were very small, so the diapers and clothes I had brought were much too big. While holding you, I felt that your diaper was wet. You had just arrived after a four-hour train ride from your orphanage. I did not want to frighten you so I decided that you would be okay for a little while. I'm sure that you had been wet many times in the orphanage and were used to waiting a long time to be changed. Well, I sat down and placed you on my leg and my pant leg was immediately soaked. It was at that moment that I knew I was a mom.

Not only did I change your diaper, but I had to change your shirt, your t-shirt, your pants, and my pants. After I changed you (and me), I tried to have you pull yourself up while holding my hands from lying on the bed, but you were unable to pull yourself to a sitting position. It was a little concerning. The Social Welfare Institute's medical report said that you could sit up and pull yourself up to standing. So we wondered if something was wrong, but we did not worry too much. We figured that the orphanage's report was incorrect. We understood that that happens sometimes.

You were very tired and warm. It was very hot in the city, probably in the high 80s with a lot of humidity. We just thought you were exhausted from your trip and meeting your new family. And perhaps you were hot because it was just plain hot in the hotel. The air conditioning in our hotel room wasn't working very well. So I put on your pajamas, took out your pigtails and attempted to feed you. You should have been starving. It must have been at least six hours since you had last ate. But you rejected the bottle. You pushed the bottle of formula away many times and turned your head away. I tried different nipples, different temperatures, different consistencies, but you would have none of it. I did not push it. I assumed that refusing to eat was one way you were coping with the tremendous stress of losing your caregivers and meeting a new family (strangers to you). Soon after I gave up feeding you, you fell asleep. You slept through the night by my side. You were quiet most of the night, but a few times you would thrash your head back and forth while you were still asleep. I would just touch your hair and you calmed and returned to a peaceful sleep.

The next morning you woke up happy and ready to go. We went downstairs to get breakfast at the hotel's buffet. Again you refused all food: you pushed away the bottle, pursed your lips against congee (Chinese rice cereal), and turned your head to avoid a slice of banana. You were more interactive and liked seeing the other girls from your orphanage in the hotel restaurant. You stood up on my lap and watched everyone else eat but you ate nothing. After breakfast, it was time to officially make you my daughter. Before we left for the adoption proceedings, I took your temperature (you felt warm to me); it was 100 degrees Fahrenheit, which was a little high but nothing to worry about. So off we went to adopt you. We loaded into a van (with no air conditioning) with many other families. Unfortunately, there wasn't enough room in the van for your grandparents to go with us, so it was just you, your aunt, and me. It was a tight fit and everyone was tired and hot. It was 9:00 a.m. and it was already eighty degrees and humid. And of course very few families got sleep last night as they tried to soothe their crying babies, or they were wide awake because their bodies were still on U.S. time (China is twelve hours ahead of Eastern Standard Time), or they just couldn't stop gazing at their baby that they had waited a lifetime to have. The van was filled with frightened, anxious, uneasy, excited, crying, sleeping, and joyful babies and parents.

When we arrived at our first stop (the certification office), you were getting warmer and lethargic. You were continuing to refuse food, crying even when I just brought a bottle into your view. It took about two hours for the paperwork to be processed at the certification office for us and the other families. The office was one room about the size of a typical U.S. school classroom. It had hard wooden benches and, of course, no air conditioning and no windows. The government officials sat at a large conference table at the front of the room. They called up one family at a time to complete the paperwork. You and I were the second to last family called. You were hot and very cranky. Your hair was getting wet from sweat.

By the time we loaded into the van for our second drive you were very warm and exhausted. I fanned you with a calendar the certification office gave us with pictures of girls adopted from the Guangxi Province, which is where you were from. I told our adoption facilitator, Shelly, that you were getting worse, but she told me that you just had a "little cold" and to give you Tylenol when we got back to the hotel. Our next stop was the notary office. You were feeling much worse by then. You were very hot and fussy; it was probably ninety degrees outside with no air conditioning in the office. The notary office was even smaller than the certification office. We were crammed into a small room and the hallway outside. We waited for our turn. With your wilting body cradled in my arms, I signed the paperwork and put my red-inked thumbprint on your adoption certificate. I was officially your mom. It was a wonderful moment—I think. I really don't remember feeling exalted because I was so worried about you. You were getting sicker and sicker and no one would listen (or maybe no one understood) and no one would acknowledge the urgency of your condition.

We arrived back to the hotel and the moment we stepped out of the van I again told the adoption facilitator, Shelly, that you were ill. I tried to explain in English that you were dehydrated, very flaccid, and had no strength. The facilitator's English was good but I am not sure that she understood me. I was persistent and kept insisting that you were very sick and needed help. Finally the adoption facilitator asked to hold you. Once she had you in her arms she immediately called for the hotel doctor to come to our room to look at you.

The hotel doctor came up immediately. Before she arrived, Shelly and our other adoption facilitator, Ellen, tried to get you to drink some water out of a bottle. As they brought the bottle near to your mouth, you arched your back and screamed. With you almost lifeless in my arms, I was glad to see that you had some fight in you when they tried to force you to eat. Their attempt to get you to take water from your bottle was unsuccessful. The doctor talked to the adoption facilitators and checked your temperature. The doctor did not even touch you. I could not understand anything that they were saying. It was so difficult not knowing what was going on. The doctor told us that you needed to go to the hospital right away. I was so worried and scared. Your aunt packed a bag with toys, diapers, a bottle and formula, your clothes, and two blankets. The adoption facilitator told us to bring two blankets, one to put over you and one to put under you and your head. Shelly, Ellen, me, your aunt, and of course you, all piled into a taxi and headed to the Nanning Women and Children's Hospital.

With you lying limp in my arms like a rag doll, I held on tightly as our taxi driver darted in and out of high speed traffic, honking at and barely missing a few bicyclists and pedestrians, and running through a few red lights. I'm not sure why they had stop lights in China; they were rarely obeyed. After a nail-biting taxi ride, we safely pulled up to the hospital. It was a four-story building that was very inviting, with brightly colored streamers in the front entrance. It was a greyish, cement building with an open design. The hospital was in the middle of a bustling small southern Chinese city that had an almost tropic climate (very similar to southern Florida). It was very hot and humid and the hospital had no cooling system. The hospital must have been constructed to optimize its ability to remain as cool as possible. The hospital had many openings in the walls for windows but no window panes. To navigate from one area of the hospital to another, we often went outside along a walkway. The patient rooms had no doors. As a matter of fact, the hospital only had a few doors. I only remember doors at the entrance, a door on the x-ray room, and doors on the bathrooms. It was very different from the hospitals in the United States.

The first hundred feet of the hospital was a hallway lined on one side with cashiers behind glass. We had to pay first before we could be seen by the emergency room doctor. I think I paid 40 yuan (5 US dollars in 2001). We walked to the emergency room. It was actually one room: an empty room with no medical equipment or supplies. The room could not have been more than eight feet square. There was only one doctor sitting at a wooden desk and one cloth cot on the back wall. We only had to wait a few minutes on a bench outside the room in the hallway. The adoption facilitator took you into the room with me in tow. I felt helpless and unable to help you. I did not understand the language, the hospital process, the medicine, the culture, or you.

The emergency room doctor talked with the adoption facilitator, Shelly, and examined you. He checked your temperature with a glass mercury thermometer under your arm; it was 38 degrees Celsius (only slightly elevated), which is 100.4 degrees Fahrenheit. He looked in your mouth and found your throat and tongue covered with white spots. He looked at your body and listened to your heart and lungs with a very old stethoscope. He then sent us to get blood work done. He gave the adoption facilitator a written order and we went down the hall to get your blood drawn. We walked into a small room where a person sat at a counter behind a small window protected by black metal bars. This medical technician reached through the bars of the window, grabbed your tiny middle finger, wiped it clean and then cut your finger with a razor. It was all very quick and rather frightening. You screamed. The technician gathered your drops of blood and then left us there to wait. The technician returned a few minutes later and handed the adoption facilitator a paper with lots of numbers and writing that I couldn't understand. We walked the results back to the emergency room doctor. Your white blood count was very high. The doctor told the facilitator, who then translated for me, that you had a serious infection and you were dehydrated. The doctor insisted that you needed to be treated and admitted to the hospital immediately. I was very worried but also relieved that you were finally going to get the help you needed.

In order to admit you to the hospital we had to return to the cashiers in the front hallway. I had to prepay for your care. I gave them 400 yuan ($50 U.S. Dollars). You were assigned to bed 38 on the third floor of the hospital. It was the first room to the left of the elevator and right next to the nurses' station. The room was large and had two oversized beds. Your roommate was a four-month-old boy. I'm not sure what was wrong with him, because everyone in the hospital had "just a little cold." Your bed was next to a doorway that led out to a small terrace. The terrace had a sink and behind a door in a very tiny room (two by two feet) was a squat toilet (I only had to use it once, thank goodness).[1] There was running water in the sink but we could not drink it. So twice a day volunteers brought a blue canister full of boiling hot water with a cork in the top. We made your formula with that water. Your bed was a large twin bed. The bed was clean but we were told that the hospital only changed sheets between patients. So, we put the quilt that your aunt had made for you under you, with a portion of it folded up for a pillow. It was a beautiful hand-stitched quilt with a rocking horse made from purple and pink polka-dotted fabric. Your grandmother had given you a handmade crocheted pink baby blanket that we covered you with.

Once we got you settled into bed, you just lay there quietly. It seemed like it took the hospital staff forever to come into your room but I'm sure that it wasn't long. Finally, a nurse came in to start an IV to transfuse fluids and to give you a shot in your little bottom to decrease your high temperature. Because I couldn't communicate with you or the nurse, the adoption facilitator, Ellen, held you. Ellen stayed with us throughout your hospital stay. You were so sick that you didn't have any reaction to having the IV placed in the top of your hand; you just lay there, quiet and motionless. It was scary. The nurse was amazing. She very quickly poked your very small hand and got the IV in on her first try. They secured the IV to your hand and arm with an old empty cardboard medicine box and some tape. It worked just fine. The "sugar water" (fluid and nutrients) was in a glass IV bottle on a pole near your bed. The hospital's equipment and procedures were like those used more than thirty years ago in the United States. It was like stepping back into time.

Once you were stable, your aunt left the hospital and returned to the hotel to tell your grandparents what was happening and to bring back food for Ellen and me. Shelly had returned to the hotel earlier because one of the families in our travel group had lost their passport (it was found later). So your aunt was on her own; she had to find her way back to the hotel by herself. She showed the taxi driver the business card for the hotel and he safely got her to the hotel. After your aunt assured your grandparents that you were safe and getting much needed treatment, she again, all by herself, returned to the hospital (after another terrifying taxi ride). She brought food for us. Ellen and I were so grateful for a Chinese muffin and cheese crackers. It was getting late in the day and we had eaten breakfast many, many hours before; we were starving. I was also so relieved to have someone to talk to in English. No one in the hospital spoke English and Ellen's English skills were very limited. As your aunt and I talked, your fragile body lay quiet and motionless on the quilt that your aunt had made for you.

During the first few hours of treatment you slept quietly. You had a fever, but the nurses had you covered up with your grandmother's blanket. You kept kicking it off, but the nurses insisted that you had to be covered, so I kept putting it back on. Ellen and I took turns running our fingers through your sweat-drenched hair, hoping that would cool you off a little. About two hours into your treatment a nurse came in with a needle and a glass syringe with some medicine in it and wanted to put it in your arm. I, of course, wanted to know what she was doing to you. Ellen tried to use her limited English to explain to me what the nurse was going to do, but I couldn't understand. Ellen kept saying that it "is an experiment." I was alarmed; what experiment? After much miscommunication I finally figured out that the nurse wanted to test medicine (penicillin) on your arm to make sure you were not allergic to it. Now understanding the situation, I let the nurse do her "experiment." You did not have an allergic reaction and so the nurse pushed penicillin into your IV bottle with a syringe.

After one bottle of "sugar water" and a dose of penicillin through your IV, the nurses asked us to try to get you to drink water from your bottle. Tears streamed down my face as you drank from the bottle for the first time since you were put into my arms. It was in that moment that I knew you would be okay. As I was drying my tears, eight nursing students came in to see you. The Nanning Women and Children's Hospital was a teaching hospital. They chatted with Ellen and said how beautiful you were and told her to tell me that you would be fine.

Later that afternoon, once you were awake a bit, we took you into a treatment room down the hallway. This room had four wooden chairs in front of five-foot tall tanks of oxygen, a small tray table with respiratory masks and medicine, and two treatment tables where other infants were getting IVs that were put into a vein in their heads. You were there for a respiratory treatment to help you breathe better. Each day you were at the hospital, you and I went to this treatment room. Every day we had an audience. There were only three or four other children and their parents in the treatment room with us, but there was always a crowd of people in the hallway peering around both sides of the door frame. They would quickly disperse when you finished your treatment and we returned to your room. I wish I knew what they were thinking and saying to one another. The hospital was in the center of a very poor and developing city in the south of China. You and I were quite a sight. You were a very little and very sick orphan. You were also not one of them; you looked different. You were beautiful and petite with dark skin and large eyes and long hair. Shelly, our adoption facilitator, believed that you were probably from a tribal minority from the southern border of China. Then there was me, a very white, very tall (almost six feet), and very thin American woman holding you. I might have been the first white American the people at the hospital had ever seen. The two of us, together in these very difficult circumstances, certainly were conspicuous. Everyone was curious and wanted to see us, much like a circus sideshow. I'm sure the hospital was buzzing.

The nurses came in every hour to check your temperature. They used a glass mercury thermometer under your arm. We held it there for five minutes. You were so sick you didn't even care and you lay very still. Your temperature kept going down. A good sign. They also gave you "baby tea" to fight your fever. It was an herbal eastern medicine, a powder that we mixed with hot water and which you drank through your bottle. You got two ounces of "baby tea" every four hours. You loved it and it kept your fever down, so I loved it, too.

It was after seven o'clock in the evening and I started making plans to stay the night at the hospital with you. Ellen suggested that I return to the hotel to get some rest and she would stay with you. Well, of course, that was out of the question; I would never leave you. So Shelly asked your grandparents, who were back at the hotel waiting for news about you, to pack an overnight bag for me so that I could stay with you. A half an hour later, Shelly arrived at the hospital with bathrobes, toothbrushes, and contact cleaner, but no glasses or clothes. Fortunately, thirty minutes later, after your temperature stayed down for a couple of hours, the hospital let me sign you out AMA (against medical advice). They let you "go home" to the hotel every night as long as I gave you "baby tea" every four hours, checked your temperature regularly, and agreed to immediately return you to the hospital if you jumped a temp or got worse. I had to sign a document that said I was taking you from the hospital against medical advice; or at least I think that was what I was signing. It was written in Chinese characters and of course I couldn't read it. I signed it, then bundled you up and grabbed a taxi back to the hotel. You rested well that night. I was exhausted. It had been an emotional and physically demanding day: the celebration of your adoption, the stress of your illness, the fear of your unknown future, the inability to communicate, my compassion for you as you underwent treatment, the lack of sleep, the very little food, and on and on.

For the next three mornings, you and I, along with Ellen, the adoption facilitator, rose early and headed back to the hospital for treatment. On the second day at the hospital, you were medically stable, so the doctor ran some tests to find out what was wrong. Your doctor was a woman who was one of the top doctors at the hospital. She ordered an x-ray and EKG. As we were waiting with many other families for the elevator to go to get your x-ray, the director of your Social Welfare Institute (orphanage) arrived. He was a young man, rather tall, and had a medium build. He brought you flowers and a red envelope with money in it. Ellen explained that it is very rare that a Chinese hospital would allow flowers; they believed that they could bring disease. It was a beautiful bouquet with yellow, red, and purple flowers, baby's breath, pink tissue paper, and a dark purple ribbon. The red envelope is a tradition in China to give to a child when they are sick. It had a few pieces of Chinese money equal to about three or four U.S. dollars. The adoption facilitator said that the money was to wish you a speedy recovery and to help me pay for your hospital care. I remember the director of the orphanage saying in English, "Sorry, sorry, sorry." The adoption facilitator said that he must have known that you were sick while at the Social Welfare Institute. Our elevator arrived so we had to go. It was a short visit but I was grateful that the director drove four hours to make sure you were all right and to apologize. He left your flowers and the red envelope in your room and returned home. He obviously cared for you.

We sat on a bench in the hallway waiting for your turn in radiology. You were awake but very lethargic. We sat near another family who must have been waiting for an x-ray as well. It was a little boy and his parents. I would say that the boy was about two or three years old. He sat on his mom's lap and had split pants on. Split pants are pants that are not sewn shut in the crotch. All the babies and young children were wearing them. The young infants in the hospital had split pants on but had a pad tied with a string around the waist that covered their crotch area (like a diaper). The kids wore split pants so that they could go to the bathroom as they needed. So this little boy was sitting quietly on his mom's lap when I saw a stream of yellow "water" arching up into the air and sprinkling onto the floor. No one reacted, no one said anything, and no one cleaned it up. People walked around it or through it. I was stunned. The hospital was so different from U.S. hospitals. Talk about culture shock.

After waiting only a few minutes, it was your turn for an x-ray. A large wooden sliding pocket door opened and we entered a room with a fairly modern x-ray machine and one technician. He positioned you on the table and took two x-rays. I stood in the corner of the room with the adoption facilitator, completely unprotected from the radiation. We then went into the next room and a technician did an EKG. Again, I felt like I was stepping back into time. The EKG machine had six bulb electrodes that she suctioned onto your chest and the readout was drawn by a colored pen on a paper strip. Even though the tests were outdated by U.S. standards, the doctors got the information they needed to save your life. The doctor diagnosed you with dehydration, severe malnutrition (you weighed only twice as much as a newborn baby and you were almost one year old), a bacterial infection of the throat, and pneumonia. Wow, scary.

Your second day at the hospital was a busy one. Your aunt and grandparents came to visit after lunch. They were very glad to see you and very curious about the hospital. It was so different from what we know in the United States. You slept the entire time they were there. About a half an hour into their visit your IV emptied and you were allowed to sign out AMA and return to the hotel with your "baby tea." So we all loaded into one taxi and went home.

Your four days at the hospital were all very similar: IV fluids and antibiotics, breathing treatment, and "baby tea." During the first day, you slept or lay motionless with exhaustion and sickness. The next three days, you were starting to feel better and wanted to be more active. Ellen and I tried to keep you entertained while confining you to the bed that you were tethered to by your IV line. It was challenging to distract you so that you wouldn't pull out the IV from your hand. We sang silly songs and soothed you with singing "la la la" to the tune of Jingle Bells; I don't know why this worked but I could hear many parents throughout the hospital singing Jingle Bells to their crying children. We looked at books, but you quickly got bored. Ellen put on puppet shows with the stuffed animals I brought to the hospital. You loved her silliness and you giggled and giggled.

On the fourth day at the hospital the doctor discharged you with "baby tea" to relieve pain and keep your temperature down, cough syrup, and powder antibiotics that I had to mix with water. This very rural hospital that used medical techniques that had been used thirty years ago in the United States and that cost me less than one hundred US dollars, saved your life!

My daughter Rose's first four days in China with me taught me the invaluable life lessons that guide me as I parent all of my children. I learned to expect the unexpected, to be persistent, to be forgiving, to be responsive, to be flexible, and to be creative. I learned to listen to my child, see life through her eyes, and respect her self-knowledge. I learned to be playful even in the most unlikely circumstances. I discovered that children, even the most vulnerable, are incredibly resilient and strong. I witnessed and gained an understanding of the importance of caring and compassion. I learned that birth-parent genetics influence my children's health and well-being. I learned how to build a bond with my daughter as she trusted me to save her life. My daughter taught me to remember what is important, to be purposeful, and to be grateful for life itself.

I often think about the difference two weeks would have made. If I had not had the opportunity to travel two weeks earlier than originally planned, what would have happened to Rose, my precious daughter? I will always be grateful for the unexpected early travel to China. It may have been the most important factor in saving Rose's life. Two weeks later may have been too late. Would the orphanage have sought medical care for Rose? Could the orphanage have afforded the medical treatment she needed? Would the rural doctors in Rose's village know how to diagnose or treat her? Would there have been the medicine she needed in her very poor community that was four hours away from the hospital that ultimately saved her? I am truly thankful for the unexpectedly rushed travel.

I had many surprises in the first few days as an adoptive parent. Rose's one-page medical report given to me two months before her adoption told me that she was a healthy child who was growing and developing normally, which was probably true at the time. Her illnesses were unanticipated; all I had hoped for on the plane ride was for a healthy child. I quickly learned to expect the unexpected and to be okay with that. I learned to adapt and act; my daughter's life depended on it.

Rose and I did not speak the same language. She had a couple of Chinese words at eleven months old and I only knew how to say hi, bye, and I love you in Mandarin (even after a year of Chinese language classes). We were strangers to one another and did not know how to read each other's non-verbal cues. Even though we had only met a few hours earlier, Rose was clearly communicating to me her needs. I just had to listen. She was screaming at me: help me! She knew she was sick. Every time she pushed the bottle away, or arched her back, or whimpered, or thrashed her head back and forth, she was talking to me. And when I didn't listen, she quickly descended into lethargy. Well, she got my attention and finally the attention of the adoption facilitators. Thank you, Rose, for telling me what you needed.

There were only two adoption facilitators (Shelly and Ellen) with twelve adoptive families. All the babies were fussy, hot, and scared and the new parents were cranky, sweltering, and anxious. We were all crammed into overflowing vans and very small government offices. The adoption facilitators were handling stacks of vital adoption paperwork, navigating complex government processes, managing highly stressed families, and listening to crying babies, all the while trying to execute very precise adoption decrees for each child and family. Is it any wonder that they dismissed my concerns regarding Rose's health? But I persisted and insisted that Rose needed help. They listened to my pleas and their actions led us to the cure. I am very grateful to Shelly and Ellen. Before we left China, my sister and I found a bag of Hershey's chocolate kisses in the hotel gift shop and gave them to Ellen and Shelly to thank them for giving Rose so many "sweet kisses" in the hospital. Rose's grandfather than gave both Ellen and Shelly real kisses on their cheeks to thank them for saving his precious new granddaughter.

I am grateful every day for Rose's aunt and grandparents. I would never have been able to care for Rose without their support and travels to and from the hospital to bring us food and to lift our spirits.

Our time at the Chinese hospital certainly had many unforeseen learning opportunities. Each nurse and doctor was caring and compassionate. The doctor responsible for Rose's care was to be on vacation after her first day of treatment, but she came into the hospital every day to treat Rose. Her self-sacrifice and devotion to Rose's well-being was admirable. I brought small gifts of thanks to the hospital for the doctors and nurses. It was customary to give small tokens of appreciation in China. I had brought a dozen small gifts including a key ring, note paper, and a local college t-shirt to give to Rose's orphanage caregivers and director and to give to the adoption facilitators. But I had already given these gifts. So Grandma and Rose's Aunt looked through the things that we had brought and found four things I could give: a deck of cards, nail polish, note cards, and chocolate. I wrapped them in some leftover red paper and a red bag and brought them to the hospital to give. The nurses and doctors were reluctant to accept these small gifts but understood my gratitude for saving Rose's life.

Before we left the hospital I asked how I could repay them (the hospital stay was less than a hundred US dollars). In the four days we spent in the hospital, I watched the doctors and nurses bring Rose back from great peril, with very limited medical resources. The emergency room had only a cot and one doctor with a stethoscope. The hospital had no running drinking water. The cardiac department had a thirty-year-old EKG machine. They used glass IV bottles, a razor blade to take blood, and an empty medicine box to stabilize an IV. The adoption facilitator asked the doctor what the hospital needed. This was a large children's teaching hospital and they did not have an otoscope (a simple medical device used to look into the ear), a basic tool that every doctor takes for granted in the United States. After we arrived home, I purchased an otoscope and sent it to the hospital with the next family that was traveling to Nanning, China. Ironically I sent it with a family that I was originally scheduled to travel with. I will never be able to repay the hospital. I am forever indebted to the hospital's doctors and nurses for saving Rose's life.

After the initial shock of Rose's medical status and the whirlwind of seeking treatment, I had become angry at the orphanage director, at Rose's birth parents, and at the Chinese government. I was furious at the director of the orphanage. He had to have known that Rose was sick. Why didn't he get her treatment; was he going to let her die? The adoption facilitator had tried to explain to me that the orphanage was very poor and probably did not have the money needed for medicine and the director knew I was coming—the rich American—and that I would get Rose the care she needed. After meeting the orphanage director outside the elevators at the hospital, I softened and accepted his heart-felt apology and flowers. I was also upset with Rose's birth parents. I knew that they could have never anticipated that Rose's life would one day be in danger, but they abandoned her. They left her, not knowing if she would live or die. But if they had not laid her at the crossing of West Street, she may not be alive today and would not be my daughter. They saved her. Not only did I forgive them but I thank them. I will always be grateful to them for the precious gift of my daughter. My most obscure anger was directed at China itself. I needed someone to be mad at. The government's one-child policy, the society's patriarchal structure, the country's extreme rural poverty, the lack of social services, and the devaluation of orphaned children all contributed to my daughter's story. I understood these vast influences and it took time to forgive, but I have.

On a much lighter note, I also learned to be playful and to giggle even in the most difficult of circumstances. I can still visualize Ellen, the adoption facilitator who stayed at the hospital with us, trying her best to keep Rose entertained and distracted during our long days at the hospital. She sang silly songs that made Rose smile. She and I read the same books over and over. Rose's favorite book was one in which she was able to open flaps to find a surprise underneath. We had the most fun when Ellen used the top of Rose's diaper bag as a stage and made up puppet shows using two stuffed bears I had brought to the hospital. She was very creative, and she made the very stressful experience of being in the hospital fun and silly. Thanks, Ellen!

When I first met Rose outside the elevators, I knew she was my daughter; but she was a stranger in my arms. Like all adoptive parents, I was hoping to have that "falling in love" moment the instant I met her. Of course that rarely happens. I certainly felt an overwhelming sense of motherhood and care for her. But it was unrealistic to believe that there would be love at first sight for me or for Rose. Feelings of love and attachment develop over time. The reality was that Rose was someone I needed to get to know and Rose needed to trust me in order to develop a sense of security and bonding with me. In Rose's case it was like attachment on steroids. She needed to trust that I would meet her needs and save her life. Her life depended on me. During those four days in the Chinese hospital, Rose and I bonded very quickly.

Every parent feels purposeful. We have a reason to get up every day: our children need us. Rose needed me. I had the ultimate purpose, to ensure that Rose lived. There is no greater purpose. The overwhelming pile of adoption paperwork, the wrinkled pants I was wearing, the little boy's puddle of pee, the speedy cab driver, the stares of strangers, the unchanged hospital bed sheets, the power bar lunches every day; none of that mattered. The only matter of importance was Rose's welfare.

After four days in the hospital and a few months of recovery at home, Rose proved to everyone that she can rebound from a very hard beginning in life. As I reflect back on Rose's early start in a rural, impoverished orphanage and her battle to beat her early illnesses, I am in awe of her capacity to be resilient and I am very proud of her accomplishments. Now fourteen years after her hospitalization in China, Rose is a compassionate, kind, generous, loving, silly, creative, and intelligent young woman who has changed, and will continue to change, the world.

During dinner one night, Rose and her sister and brother were talking about what their lives would be like if they had not been adopted. Her sister and brother had interesting answers, but Rose had a very simple, yet profound answer: "I'd be dead."

Expect the Unexpected

LESSON ONE

When I asked my children what the most important lesson is that they have taught me, they agreed it was to expect the unexpected (and be okay with that). My life plan has certainly taken many twists and turns that were never expected. As a child, I dreamt about finishing school, getting married, living in a beautiful home, excelling in my career, having two healthy children and being happy. My real life, however, looks very different from my childhood plan. I did finish school and I have a rewarding career. I'm not married. I have 4 children (2 more than dreamed of) who have all joined my family through adoption.

Each of us has life plans, dreams, and hopes. We have expectations for what our life will be like. The overwhelming majority of us, as we consider our adulthood, envision parenting a child or some children. We expect to be able to have a child. Almost all families who are formed through adoption, are very unexpectedly unable to have a biological child and thus choose adoption as a way to become parents. Infertility or not having a partner is the beginning of many unexpected adjustments in the life plan of an adoptive family.

Although the fostering or adopting of a child takes much planning, most adoptions are unexpected and all foster placements are surprising. One of the first things social workers counsel prospective foster/adoptive parents about is the unpredictability in adoption and the uncertainty of fostering. As adoptive parents we research our options, consult with adoption specialists, read adoption literature, and talk with other adoptive parents before we then make a very carefully constructed plan for our future family. You can make an adoption plan or set parameters for foster care. As a matter of fact, your social worker (including me) will ask you to detail your plans. For example, you may say that you wish to parent a healthy female child, no older than three, from the country of South Korea; or that you want to adopt a school-aged boy with special needs from China; or that you hope to adopt a newborn child, who is healthy, from the United States; or that you are prepared to foster a sibling group of three children who are all under the age of five. These plans provide the framework from which you build your family or offer foster care. However, no one can predict who your child will be, how the child will enter your family, from where your child will come, or when your dreams of having a child will become a reality. Some families' adoption and foster care journeys lead them quickly down the straight and narrow path. Other journeys lead families around the corner, over the mountain, down into the valley, into the forest, and through a fork in the road. Those families who forge ahead and embrace the experience come to the beginning of a new adventurous journey: parenthood.

Adoptive and foster parenting holds many surprises, which are both joyous and challenging. Each of us has expectations for our dreamed-of child: she will be artistic, he will be funny, she will be athletic, he will be studious, she will be a leader, and so on; but who will our child really become? In the wild adventure of parenthood, there will always be the joyous discovery of your child's interests, talents, and aspirations. There will also be the challenge of unknown birth family history, loss of birth family (and birth culture for some kids), and possibly baffling medical conditions or learning differences. There is the joy of your child's first step, his first day at school, and you hearing Mama or Dada for the first time. There is the challenge of helping your child develop a positive sense of self in relation to adoption (and race for some kids). There is the joy of cheering at your daughter's baseball game or enjoying your child's band concert. There is the task of uncovering special learning needs. There is the pleasure of discovering a special talent. There is the challenge of supporting your child's emotional needs as a result of a traumatic history. There is the excitement of helping your child to learn how to read. Every day brings new insights and new delights.

Parenting through adoption and foster care necessitates us to rewrite the blueprint of our lives. It requires us to modify our life plan and alter our expectations. It also gives us the freedom to expect the unexpected, and be okay with that.

Two Care Packages
Marco, adopted in 2007 at 10 months of age

I was working as a social worker in an adoption agency that occasionally collaborated with an international adoption placement agency. I was parenting your two sisters. I had just finished graduate school and we had recently moved into a new house and community. We were getting settled and I was comfortable in my life. Then the international adoption placement agency called asking if I knew of any families who would be open to adopting an older male infant from Guatemala. He was only nine months old, but this was considered older for Guatemalan adoption at the time. I thought, this should be easy. I searched for two months to find a family, calling everyone who might be a resource for this little boy. But no one would adopt Carlos. So, I called the international adoption placement agency and told them that I would be his mom. They agreed and as quickly as I could, I got my home study investigation completed, obtained my pre-approval from the U.S. Citizenship and Immigration Service to adopt a foreign-born orphan, and submitted my application (known as a dossier) to Guatemala for consideration for Carlos.

Everything was proceeding as planned. My paperwork was sailing through the government processes and it looked like Carlos would be home soon. I sent a care package filled with toys, clothes, and books to Carlos. A worker from the adoption agency was traveling to Guatemala, so she took the package to his foster home for me. I couldn't wait to hear how Carlos was doing after the worker visited him and gave him the toys I sent. But days after her visit I had still had heard nothing. I wondered if something was wrong. Then my co-worker came to me, and told me that Carlos' birth mother had returned and decided to parent Carlos. I was devastated. In my mind, Carlos was already my son. He was in my new life plan. I respected his birth mother's decision and was glad that Carlos was able to remain in his birth family. However, I was very sad that I would not be his mother. The excitement and anticipation of this unexpected adoption became the hurt of the unexpected loss of his adoption.

The adoption agency gave me time to grieve and reevaluate my adoption plans. Well, actually they gave me two days. Then again, very unexpectedly, the adoption agency called and said that they had another little boy, only two months old, who needed a family. They explained that he may have been born early, but they did not know for sure. All they knew was that he weighed only five pounds at one month old. The agency sent me pictures of you, and you were adorable. I quickly said yes and began paper chasing again. I put together another care package filled with clothes, toys, books, and a blanket, and sent it to your foster family. Your foster mother sent me back pictures of you surrounded by the toys and wearing the clothes. Every month, I received new pictures of you and a quick medical update. You were growing up too fast. I desperately wanted you home. Seven months later, after many paperwork glitches, governmental regulatory changes, unexplained delays, and the United States threatening to close down adoption in Guatemala, you arrived safely home the week after Easter. You were one of the last children permitted out of Guatemala before the United States closed to inter-country adoption from your country.

I still think of Carlos and hope he and his family are well. I always thank Carlos for bringing us together. My unplanned adoption of Carlos, became my unexpected adoption of you.

Just for a Couple of Weeks
Kyle, fostered at 6 years of age

On a Thursday afternoon, I got a call from a caseworker from the Department of Social Services. The caseworker explained that your single mother was going into the hospital to give birth to your brother and had nowhere for you to stay while she was away. She had no friends or family who could care for you. So your mother asked Social Services to place you in temporary foster care for just a couple of weeks. Social Services told me that you were a healthy child who did well in school and had no known behavioral or emotional problems. It was my first call to provide foster care and I gladly said "sure."

You were six years old with reddish-brown hair and freckles. You were cute. You were very bright. You were silly, charming, and mischievous. Well, two weeks went by very quickly. Your brother was born and your mother and baby brother were settled into home. I expected for you to return home to your mom and new brother. That did not happen; that never happened.

After a couple of weeks, your mother and baby brother did start to visit you at my home. Your mom was a sweet woman who I liked very much. Your brother was adorable. Your mom and I developed a very good relationship over the next six months. I learned so many things from your mom. It was true that she asked for you to be voluntarily placed into foster care because she was having a baby. However, she did have family and friends, but all refused to care for you. Even though she would be in the hospital for only two days, she asked for more time because she was afraid that you would hurt the new baby. Your mother was very smart to protect your baby brother from you.

I quickly learned from your mom and from your actions that although you were a healthy child who was very smart, you had behaviors that were frightening. You could be destructive and violent. You would often go into an unprovoked rage and trash your room.

Many things got broken or ruined. Your room eventually just had a bed. I had to remove all else to protect you and your things. You could be very manipulative and charming to get around the rules of the house and school. If you didn't get your way, you would attack. You wet your bed every night and then would wake up and make designs on the wall with your urine stream. I tried everything to curb this behavior but nothing worked. Your behaviors were disturbing. Your mother was very worried that one day you may harm someone or yourself. I must admit that I, too, was worried.

Over the next six months, I tried many things to help you: counseling, medication, and behavior modification, but nothing seemed to have an impact. I did not know how to help you. I felt helpless and hopeless. I felt like a failure. But I also knew that you needed a higher level of care than what I could provide. Your mother, the Department of Social Services, and I all agreed that you needed to be moved into a therapeutic foster home. Six months after you came to my house, you moved to an experienced therapeutic foster care home. I understand that you lived there for two months, but they also were not able to meet your needs. Your mom told me that they moved you to a behavioral health center for youth. I think of you often and hope you are safe and happy.

Pickles
Wu LeBin, adopted in 2015 at almost 8 years of age

I was very excited to add to my family through the adoption of an older child with special needs from China. I wanted to have another son, and your sisters and brother were excited to have another brother. I was confident in my ability to parent another child with minor special needs. It was Friday afternoon, and I noticed your profile on an adoption agency's website featuring older children with special needs. You were the last child pictured on the site because you were given the English name of Wade. You caught my eye. I called the adoption agency and asked about adopting. I asked them about a couple of boys listed on their site waiting for a family. Then they asked me to consider you, the last little boy on their list. You were almost six years old and had an arm and hand deformity. I thought I could easily parent a child with such a minor concern. The adoption caseworker gave me your medical report, a few pictures, and a very short video of you running around a playroom which gave me a quick look at your arm deformity. Your medical report was from when you were only nine months old, and only stated that you had a right-side arm and hand deformity. I asked the adoption agency for a current medical report. According to the adoption agency, the orphanage refused to get a new medical report, stating that you were a healthy child. The adoption agency explained that the orphanage didn't want to pay for a medical exam because you were a healthy child with only a limb deformity. I took your medical report, pictures, and video to a pediatrician who was familiar with limb deformities, and who worked for a medical practice with expertise in international adoption. The doctor reviewed the information and confirmed your radial dysplasia (arm and hand deformity).[2] I asked if you could have a syndrome related to this deformity. He explained that you did not have any other features or medical issues that would be consistent with a syndrome. The doctor told me that your limb deformity was an isolated issue and that you appeared to be a typical kid.

I took your sisters and brother out to dinner at a Chinese restaurant to celebrate Chinese New Year and to talk to them about the possibility of adopting another child into our family. Your siblings were thrilled to learn about you and all agreed that it was a great idea to adopt you. So after your siblings supported the adoption plan, I decided to submit my application to China for consideration to adopt you. I trusted China's medical report. I trusted the adoption agency's assessment of your needs. I trusted the medical expert's evaluation. I said "yes" to your adoption. I was very excited, but nervous because the China Center for Child Welfare and Adoption had to accept my application for your adoption. I put together an application to request pre-approval of your adoption. While we waited (approximately one month) to learn if the Chinese government would allow me to adopt you, we couldn't tell anyone—grandparents, uncles, aunts, cousins, friends—because my application could get denied by the Chinese government. So on our way home from the Chinese restaurant, your siblings were deciding on a code name for you. Your sister Pearl had a craving for pickles, so she suggested pickles and it stuck. So whenever we talked about you, you were "Pickles." Thirty days later, China approved our match, and I was permitted to proceed with your adoption. Your siblings and I were all thrilled. You were no longer Pickles; you became Wu LeBin.

Only after China pre-approved my adoption of you did I receive additional information about your medical and developmental status. There was no date on the reports, but it appeared that you might at that time have been three years old based on the number of teeth you reportedly had at the time of the evaluation. The agency could not tell me when the evaluation had occurred, but it was clearly done prior to my initial review of your file. So why wasn't it provided when I initially asked for an updated medical? These new reports were full of discrepancies. Three reports stated that you had a hand and arm deformity and no other abnormal findings while one report said you had poor abilities of adaptability, language, and social ability. So what was true? What did "poor abilities" mean and were these unspecified issues due to institutionalization or organic causes?[3] I was confused and concerned. I provided the new information to the medical practice that initially reviewed your file and they did not put up any red flags. The adoption agency did not seem concerned either. I was worried, but my suspicions were downplayed by the medical provider and adoption agency.

I remember asking if you were attending school (you were school-aged). The adoption agency told me no, but then quickly told me that children in this orphanage don't go to school until they are eight years old and you were only seven years old. So, okay, that made sense. Of course I now know that that was not true in your case; you were not attending school because you did not have the capacity to go to a school.

Then I was excited to learn that a social worker from the adoption agency had visited you in the orphanage and had a new video to share. I couldn't wait to talk with her and see the video. I got the video while watching your sister play baseball. I viewed it on my phone while in the baseball stands. You were adorable, but I had some questions. You were silent; but then no one asked you to talk. You weren't playing with the other children; but you were fascinated by the adults taking your video. You were curious, but you did not seem to show interest in others. I did not know what to think. I spoke with the social worker who visited with you. She told me that you were a busy boy who was happy and curious. You could listen and follow directions. You appeared able to have conversations. I asked about your cognitive skills (thinking and intelligential abilities). She thought you might have cognitive delays, and when I pushed her, she agreed that you may have cognitive deficits; but were they organic or situational? You were participating in preschool activities (stringing beads and identifying colors). The social worker told me that you loved chocolate treats. I specifically asked her if you had Autism Spectrum Disorder behaviors.[4] I thought I saw something in the video, but she told me no. She told me that she had observed you in the orphanage watching cartoons with a friend. Great, you had a friend (autistic children typically don't have friends). I held onto hope, knowing that you had a friend.

It was finally time to travel to China to adopt you and bring you home. Your sisters, your brother, your aunt, and I were on our way to China to meet you. Everyone was excited. We arrived at the government office and you and your caregivers were already there. Your caregiver escorted you over to me, your new sisters, and your brother, as soon as we entered the room. I crouched down, and you gave me an artificial hug at the instruction of your caregiver. You immediately turned your back to me and your new siblings (never acknowledging your sisters or brother) and stood in front of us while your aunt took pictures. You said nothing and looked at no one. I knew within those first few moments that you were significantly autistic.

Your orphanage gave you a brand new Mickey Mouse backpack full of snacks. You reached inside and pulled out copies of the pictures I had sent you of myself and your new siblings. You did point to my picture and then pointed to me and said "Mama," but again you never looked at or acknowledged your siblings. Then you raced around the room randomly. There were two other families there meeting their children for the first time. So as not to distract from their joyous unions, your aunt and I took you and your siblings into an adjoining room. It was a room full of exercise equipment. You loved it. You ran back and forth from machine to machine. You liked the motion and the moving wheels. Your sisters and brother thought it was cute; I watched as you ignored your siblings and "self-stimmed" on the spinning wheels of the exercise machines.[5]

I had to return to the government office to sign paperwork and talk with your caregivers. I asked the orphanage staff who your friends were at the orphanage, knowing the answer but hoping for a different one. They told me that you did not have friends at the orphanage and that you played alone. After your adoption, the adoption agency's worker who visited you in the orphanage revised her story from "you were watching TV with a friend" to "you were watching TV next to another child." I asked the orphanage staff if you were autistic. They, of course, did not know the English word, but they searched for it on the internet and after reading the definition of autism, they said yes! As a matter of fact, they explained that when you were four years old, you went to an institute in the capital city of your province for four months for residential treatment for autism. The orphanage staff thought I knew. I had no idea. I had suspected it, but they knew and withheld the information even after my requests to the adoption agency for clarity. I'm convinced that the orphanage staff knew that the only way you would find a forever family would be to hide the reality of your complex needs. They knew that finding a family to adopt a child with autism would be improbable and finding a family willing to adopt a child with autism and eleven other significant medical and developmental diagnoses would be impossible. The staff and doctor of your orphanage may or may not have known the extent of your challenges, but their lack of disclosure of your known challenges saved your life, by finding you a family.

Once we arrived home, you were diagnosed with many additional, previously unknown or undisclosed challenges: autism, spina bifida occulta and lower spine malformations, left hand abnormalities, cognitive deficits (aka intelligential disability), language disorder, vision problems, and a potentially life-threatening heart condition.[6] I had expected a healthy, typical boy with an arm and hand deformity. Your realities were much different. After an initial adjustment, your sisters, aunts, uncles, cousins, and grandmother were "okay with it." As a matter of fact, just last week at dinner one of your sisters said that if we could go back a year and change you into who we thought you were going to be (a typical boy with a limb difference), that she would not want to change you. I must admit, some days I am accepting of your very unexpected needs and other days I struggle with it. Sometimes expecting the unexpected, and being okay with that, is hard.

He Has Your Eyes
Marco, adopted in 2007 at 10 months of age

Your cousin Thomas looks just like your grandfather when your grandfather was a little boy. Your cousin Megan is tall like her father. Your cousin TJ has a bigger-than-life personality just like his mom. Your grandparents wonder if Thomas will grow up to be interested in math and science like his father and grandfather. Your aunt thinks that TJ gets his athletic talents from his dad. We all hope that your cousins won't develop diabetes like their parents and grandparents. Thomas is a jokester just like his dad. At many holiday gatherings, you hear your aunts, uncles, and grandparents comparing the biological children to their ancestors and wondering, "Who does she look like? Who does he take after? Will she follow in her parents footsteps? Who does he get that nose from? Where did he get that quirky smile and quick wit?" We wonder these same things for you, but don't have any answers.

You have very dark eyes just like your birth mother. We have a picture of your birth mother holding you as a baby. You share her facial features. You both have a strong square face, pitch black hair, a defined chin, small nose, and almond-shaped eyes. Behind those beautiful brown eyes, you have very unique vision differences, and I often wonder if you inherited your visual challenges from your birth mom. We know very little about her, and we know nothing about your birth father. You often wonder how tall you are going to grow. Your birth mom is only five feet tall, but is her height due to genetics or poor nutrition as a child growing up in impoverished Guatemala? And without knowing how tall your birth father is, I'm not able to give you an answer. You are tall for your age, but will you continue to grow? It's impossible to know. I also can't say if you got your sense of humor from a birth relative. You are hilarious and keep everyone laughing. It's also hard to know if your talent as a bowler is linked to a birth ancestor. I won't know if you are "following in their footsteps." I am certain, however, that your birth family is a part of you and shapes your personality, interests, aspirations, and handsome good looks.

Not knowing, although difficult, allows you to grow up without family expectations or pressures. You have the freedom to be whoever you wish to be. You don't have to like writing because your grandfather was a poet, or be extroverted like your aunt, or excel in sports because your mom was an athlete, or enjoy the outdoors because your aunt and uncle are farmers. You are who you are. You are special and unique. There is no one else like you.

As your mom, the mystery of your genetics, birth history, and birth family heritage, allows me to have the joy of discovery. I never know what to expect next. Every day I learn more about you. I have no expectations of who you are or what you will become. It is exciting to think of all the possibilities.

Life would be so much easier if we could predict what was going to happen and be able to make a plan. Of course, my daughter, who has just finished reading this chapter, said, "Then life would be boring." Parenting, particularly adoptive parenting, is full of surprises. Around every corner is something new and usually unexpected. A plan for the adoption of one child may lead you to the adoption of the child who is meant to be yours. The deep brown eyes of your child may hold secrets to his past and unanticipated challenges for the future. Two weeks can quickly turn into six months. The known special needs of your child may distract you from undisclosed life-altering disabilities. Your quiet life becomes busy and exciting as you take the lead of your children. Embrace the unexpected: it will shape who you become and enrich your life beyond measure.

Look at Life Through Their Eyes

LESSON TWO

How I would love to be able to spend even one day looking through the eyes of my children. I know they don't see the world as I do. How do they perceive, process, and respond to the world? I wish I knew what they see, how their senses process information, how they feel, and what they think. We parent our children based upon our analysis of their outward behaviors and our perceptions of their thoughts and feelings. To be able to walk in their shoes would provide me with tremendous insight into their behavior, capabilities, needs, wants, thoughts, fears, joys, and wishes. I could learn how their daily experiences affect who they are and who they wish to become. We try our best, but we will never be able to truly understand our children. We joke in my family that I can't walk in my children's shoes because my feet are so big (size 12) and theirs are so tiny (sizes 1, 6, 7, and 8). As a matter of fact, as I am writing this, my daughter Pearl just sat next to me with athletic sandals she recently bought and said, "My feet are so small," and my son Marco is sitting on the other side of me looking through colored goggles at a therapeutic light hoping for better vision. To see the world as they see it would be an invaluable gift. I wish I had magic goggles and smaller feet.

The Yellow Baseball
Marco, adopted in 2007 at 10 months of age

It was the last game of Little League baseball, and it was your turn to bat. All the parents were cheering for you, hoping for a hit before the season ended. We watched as you swung with all of your might, only to have it result in another strikeout. You slowly walked off the field with your head hung low. I think you have only hit the ball once or twice in the past three years of playing baseball. You were persistent and kept your sense of humor (most of the time). Getting ready for the next baseball season, you were at Little League baseball practice with a new coach. He threw you pitch after pitch (over fifty in all) but practice ended in frustration and defeat as you hit none of his pitches. A few days later, we found a friend of yours and his father (an Assistant Little League baseball coach) at the local park practicing baseball. The father was using yellow tennis balls for batting practice. You nervously joined in and you hit the ball—hooray!

You were born in Guatemala to a single mother who placed you into foster care, hoping you would find an adoptive family. You found my family a couple months later and came home two months before your first birthday. You were a very quiet baby who would stare intently at everyone you met with your very dark and beautiful eyes.

As a toddler you showed no interest in books. You would never sit and look at books or let me read to you. I hate to admit it, but I figured you were a boy and books just weren't important to you. When you turned three years old and then four you still ignored books and you had no interest in coloring, drawing, or painting. At four years old, you were not yet able to recognize any colors. I wondered if you were color-blind and expressed my concerns to your pediatrician, but was told that you were "with normal limits." She explained that some boys don't begin recognizing colors until they are five years old. She did a vision screening and said you passed.

You did not have any vision problems. And sure enough, right after your fifth birthday, you identified five colors. Thank goodness! I was so relieved.

You attended a preschool program and struggled to learn your alphabet, your numbers, and you still had no interest in coloring, drawing, or looking at books. The teacher assured me that you were progressing and ready for kindergarten, but I had my doubts. So in the fall, you started kindergarten and tried hard to learn, but continued to have difficulty. Your teacher had been an educator for more than thirty years and was a master teacher. She helped you learn your alphabet and numbers to twenty. But you were quickly falling behind your peers. Over the next two school years, you would make just enough progress to be advanced to the next grade level. By the end of second grade, you were reading at a kindergarten level and were only able to write a sentence using a couple words. As a matter of fact, you wrote the same sentence over and over again for every assignment. You seemed oblivious to your challenges, but I'm sure you knew you were different.

During these first four years of your education (preschool to second grade), I spoke to every teacher about my concerns. They just said that you were doing fine and were simply learning at a slower pace than your peers. I asked your reading teacher why you weren't learning to read. She felt you were improving under her expert instruction, but you needed to put more effort into learning; you needed to try harder. The reading teacher thought your only impediment to reading was your lack of trying. All your teachers told me that you had difficulty paying attention in class, were easily distractible, joked around in class, goofed around with your friends, and would often get up to sharpen your pencil multiple times a day. So I asked for the school district to complete a psycho-educational evaluation. I'm sure you can guess what the assessment results were: good cognitive skills, but extremely distractible, unfocused, and a short attention span; I was told you may have Attention Deficit Hyperactivity Disorder. Well, I was not convinced; my gut was telling me that something else was preventing you from learning and was causing your inattention.

During those same four years, I searched for an answer. Every year at your well-child physical exam, I asked questions of your pediatrician and was repeatedly told that you passed your vision screening and you were developing within normal limits. I took you to three different eye doctors, who all assured me that you had 20/20 vision (perfect) and could see all colors. You didn't need glasses; your eyes were great!

I was tired of being dismissed by the professionals in your life, so I started talking to other parents who had children with vision problems. And they all pointed me to the same doctor, an eye doctor specializing in visual processing disorders. I was a little skeptical because some of the professionals I spoke with had their doubts about this doctor who used color to improve vision, but I made an appointment for you anyway. While we waited, you started Little League baseball for the third year. And again, even with perfect batting form, you could not hit that ball. Now that you were older (8 years old), I asked what you saw when the ball was pitched to you. You explained that you would swing the bat where you thought the ball was but the ball would zig zag and wiggle towards you, and you only saw it a few seconds before it hit the catcher's glove. A few days later, you hit that yellow tennis ball in the local park with your friend's dad!

We went to see the "color doctor," the eye doctor who specialized in visual processing. It took this new eye doctor less than thirty minutes to diagnose you with multiple vision issues. We finally had answers! The doctor agreed that you have 20/20 visual acuity and your eyes are healthy. However, you had many visual problems. While your eyes may have been great, your visual neural pathways and eye muscles were not. You had a very limited visual field (tunnel vision), your two eyes did not work together (binocular dysfunction), your eyes couldn't transition from near to far (convergence insufficiency), you had difficulty with figure/ground (couldn't see the white baseball against the white sky), and your eyes fatigued very quickly. Wow, that explained so much! You immediately started vision therapy, and within nine months you had made astounding progress. You were so proud of yourself, and for the first time you thought you were smart and able to learn to read and do math. With therapy and accommodations in the classroom (e.g., eye breaks, colored filters, a personal computer) you made tremendous advances. Within one year, you gained three years of reading skills and were reading a little above grade level at the end of third grade. One day about six months into treatment, you suddenly blurted out in the car, "I can see my sister!" Your sister had sat in the seat next to you in the car for years, but for the first time you could see her with your newly discovered peripheral vision. It was very exciting.

We explained your vision challenges to your Little League Baseball coach and told him that you could hit a yellow tennis ball. So with the permission of all of the opposing coaches, your coach took a yellow highlighter and colored a baseball yellow before every game. Every time you got up to bat, the pitcher used the yellow ball and you hit it every time! You were so excited. All the other parents and I were thrilled for you. It was amazing to watch you run to first base with confidence and a smile on your face. All thanks to an innovative eye doctor, amazing baseball coaches, and a yellow baseball.

Super Powers

Wu LeBin, adopted in 2015 at almost 8 years of age

We were playing in the hotel room in China just a few days after your adoption. You and your brother were playing side by side on the floor with building toys. Earlier that day, I had bought each of you a plastic building set with interlocking tiles, gears, little teddy bears, a swing, a merry-go-round, and a motor. You could build lots of fun creations: a playground with a bear swinging in a swing, a merry-go-round that took three bears around and around, a car that drove across the floor (your favorite), and anything else created from your imagination. You and your brother loved building and rebuilding your creations. Then suddenly the calmness of your playing was interrupted. You started to scream, stomp your feet, hit the dresser with your fists, and sit on the floor kicking your feet. You couldn't communicate with us (you had very few words in your native language and no English) and we had no idea what was wrong. It was very upsetting. Then, your Aunt who traveled with us, wondered if one of your building pieces was in your brother's box. So she and I sorted each box, piece by piece, fourteen different kinds of pieces and sixty-nine pieces in all. Well, sure enough, we found one of your pieces (a tiny gear connector just a bit smaller than the size of a quarter) in your brother's box. As soon as that one piece was returned to you, you calmly put it into your box, dried your tears, stopped your stomping, punching, and kicking, and sat quietly on the bed holding onto your box and watching a Chinese cartoon.

When you do something that is unexplainable, your siblings and I simply say that it's your "Autistic Super Power." Knowing that one piece is missing amongst several is one of your many super powers. Even though you are nine years old, your language skills are that of a toddler, your academic skills are at a preschool level, and your social skills are extremely limited. But you are able to convert transformers from a car to a robot and back to a car more quickly than any accomplished engineer. You love to put together and take apart complex Lego® structures; cars and trucks are your favorite. Even if one of the tiniest Legos® is missing, a car headlight for example, you will hunt for it until you find it and put it back on the car. Just last week while at your sister's softball practice, you took apart a 225 piece Lego® truck and had every piece randomly placed on a small table. Without any instructions and without a picture or model of the truck, in less than ten minutes, you quickly put the truck back together perfectly. You love to take everything apart and then put it back together, even things that are not meant to be pulled apart. You have had many tantrums over trucks and action figures you broke into pieces that could not be repaired.

You only have about twenty-five English words and are just starting to put together two-word sentences, but you can sing. As a matter of fact, you sing almost all day long. You love Taylor Swift, Maroon Five, and any radio jingle. You hear a song or jingle on the radio and immediately sing the tune. You use nonsense words and random sounds, but the melody is perfect (another amazing super power). Your sisters and brother like to guess the song. Your favorite tunes are the theme song for Power Rangers (your favorite show) and the overture to Star Wars (which you have never seen).

You have difficulty interacting with other kids and adults, but no problem relating to animals. It is as if you have special powers to connect to animals. Your first and most important "friends" are our two cats, Grandma's cat, the neighbor's dog, the dogs that walk by us as we walk to school, and so on and so on. You are gentle and kind to the animals. One day you brought a book about kittens home from school. You sat on the kitchen floor next to our cat JoJo and showed him the book. JoJo sat next to you for thirty minutes as you turned the pages and kept showing him the picture of the kitten that looked like him. I often find you and our cat JoJo sitting next to each other on the floor of the kitchen gazing out the glass door to our backyard. Cats and dogs gravitate to you, even dogs and cats that don't normally like anyone. Your sister plays a lot of softball, and one summer evening we were in the stands cheering on the team when a family brought a new bulldog puppy to the game. They had only had the dog for a couple of weeks and said that he didn't like anyone and could be mean and aggressive. Well, there was no stopping you, and you immediately went over to the dog, petted him, and put your face right next to his. I, of course, was very worried. I quickly approached you and the dog to escort you safely away from this unpredictable animal. The dog immediately growled and barked at me as I came within ten feet of you. When I retreated, the dog turned to you and gave you a sloppy kiss on the cheek. You and the dog continued to sit next to each other at the softball games throughout the summer.

While we were visiting your grandmother for the holidays I was quietly writing in this book about your super powers; I was sitting on your grandmother's living room couch, working on a laptop computer. You, your brother, and your sister were playing next to me. I hadn't spoken a word about what I was writing, nor had you glanced at the words I was typing (even if you had, you can't read yet). I paused for a moment and looked up to find you trying to tie a blanket around your sister's shoulders like a superman cape. Then you motioned to your brother to do the same and then you had your sister tie a cape around your neck. You all then pretended to be super heroes; you would fight and then cheer for each other as you flew around the room with super powers.

I want my super power to be the ability to inhabit the minds of my children, look through their eyes, and fit into their shoes. Imagine how much easier parenting would be if I could see what they see, think what they think, and feel what they feel. To know when Wu LeBin, my child with autism and limited language skills, is physically hurt could be life-saving. To see words move across the page or to try to hit a baseball as it wiggles in and out of sight, would have saved Marco from years of failure and frustration. If I could have experienced Rose's eating pain and understood what it felt like to never experience hunger, I may have been able to prevent her feeding struggles (Rose's feeding difficulties are featured later in this book). Understanding when, why, and how Wu LeBin experiences sadness, anger, confusion, or frustration would certainty reduce the number of meltdowns.

On the flip side, it would also be great to know what makes my kids happy, excited, and inspired. To know what it feels like when Wu LeBin sings the tune "If you are happy and you know it" would let me create more happy moments for him. To have the "Ah ha! I've got it" experience when Marco figured out how to divide numbers would help me know how to teach the next concept. If I knew how it felt to hit a home run, I could help Pearl practice for the next big game. Being able to feel Rose's deep empathy for others would open my eyes to the needs of others and to her full heart. To know that one piece out of one hundred Lego® pieces is missing would help me understand Wu LeBin's anxiety, and to know where to find that one missing piece would also be really nice.

Until I develop super powers, I will just be in awe of my children's insights, thoughts, and talents. I will do my best to understand them and be flexible and creative in my response to their wants and needs. I will also marvel in the unexplainable super powers of each of my children.

Trust Leads to Bonding
LESSON THREE

Even before I met my children for the first time, I had already fallen in love with them. I had expectations for their personalities, their interests and talents, and what they would accomplish in life. I had a clear idea of how it would feel to parent my long-awaited children. I had a vision of my life with my children. I dreamt of my child melting into my arms as our eyes met for the first time and we would both fall in love instantly. I was filled with great anticipation as I prepared to meet my children for the first time. I was excited but anxious, confident but uncertain, controlled but emotional, frightened but calm, worried but filled with hope, and happy but sad for the losses that created this adoption. Through this sea of emotions my children were placed into my arms for the first time. My thoughts swirled around me. I was overwhelmed by my thoughts and feelings and was in awe of this surreal moment.

In that same moment, my child was placed into the arms of a stranger: my arms, the arms of their new mommy. The child that I was desperate to love and to be loved by, was now on my lap crying, hitting, kicking, and trying to escape my embrace, or for one of my children, unresponsive in my arms. I have turned my new child's life upside down. Who was I and where did their first "mommy" go? I didn't look like their beloved caregiver from the orphanage or foster home. I didn't speak their language. I'm sure that I smelled funny and ate weird foods. Who was I to take them away from their past life so abruptly? My child had just lost everything they had ever known. They must have been confused, worried, sad, terrified, anxious, disoriented, grief stricken, and distressed. And all I wanted was for them to love me.

I learned to be patient. My new child and I were strangers. We needed time to get to know each other and to build a bond with one another. Each of my children needed to develop confidence and trust that I would consistently meet their physical, emotional, and social needs. Most people believe that attachment comes from love. However, attachment grows from trust and results in the feelings of love and bonding.[7] A child only becomes attached to you after you have repeatedly met your child's needs. Luckily, children have needs all day every day so you have thousands of opportunities to satisfy your child's needs and earn their trust. When my children are hungry, they need to know that I will always feed them. If my children are tired, they need to be assured that I will help them calm down and rest. When my children are frightened, they need to be confident that I will chase away the scary monsters in their closet before bed each night. If my children are cold, they need to be certain that I will cuddle them to warm them up after playing in the snow. When my teenager struggles to get a project done on time, she needs to believe that I will be patient, understanding, and encouraging. By consistently meeting my children's needs, my children learn to trust that I will always be there for them. And from their trust in me, feelings of attachment develop.

Most foster and adoptive parents understand the importance for their child to develop a secure attachment and appreciate that it will take time for their child to bond with them. However, most parents expect that they will instantaneously become bonded with their new child. Just like it takes time for a child to attach to his/her new parents, it also takes foster and adoptive parents time to bond with their new child. Remember, this child is a stranger to you, too. Although we all wish to fall in love at first sight, it is unrealistic to expect to immediately fall in love with our child. Just like our children, we need time to develop an attachment. We need our children to need us, and we need to become confident in our ability to meet our child's needs. We need to experience feelings of accomplishment, competency, and fulfillment in parenting. We need to experience joyful feelings as our children give us positive feedback with a smile, a hug, giggles, a thank you, a joke, etc.

Building a mutually secure attachment with your child is critical to your child's well-being and to your capacity to parent. Attachment is a process and takes time for both the child and for the parent.

Velcro Baby
Marco, adopted in 2007 at 10 months of age

Your Great Aunt Nila and I got up very early that morning and arrived at the airport at 4:30 a.m. We were already exhausted, and the day had yet to start. The plane was to depart at 6:30 in the morning. We were to arrive in Guatemala City by 2:00 in the afternoon, and then meet you before dinner. Sounds like a great plan and easy, right? Well, none of that happened. We boarded the plane at 6:00, but the plane's door would not close properly. So we waited an hour on the plane for it to be repaired, but to no avail. We were asked to get off the plane and patiently wait for another plane to arrive. Patiently wait? How? I had to be in Guatemala to meet you! The airline did have another flight going our way, but it was full. I pleaded with the airline ticket manager and explained that you were waiting for us in Guatemala City, and if we didn't get our connecting flight in Atlanta, you (and I) would need to wait another entire day and all the adoption appointments, including our appointment at the U.S. Embassy, would have to be changed. I must have looked desperate, because the person taking boarding passes at the gate boarded the plane and explained my situation to the passengers and offered anyone who volunteered to give up their seats free airline tickets to anywhere in the country. A few minutes later two young men came down the ramp and told us to have a great trip and congratulations on my adoption. Wow, what amazing kindness and self-sacrifice. We quickly thanked the men and boarded the plane, which was taxiing to the runway in five minutes.

We landed in Atlanta with thirty minutes to catch our next flight. Because we were now getting onto an international flight, we had to go through security again. For some reason we must have looked suspicious, because they searched our bags and dusted them for drugs and explosives. Then we had five minutes to board. Yes, like you see in the movies, we ran for it. We made it! We settled into our seats and were glad for some time to relax. Believe it or not, the pilot got on the intercom and announced that the plane was experiencing some mechanical problems, and the take-off was delayed. Two hours later we took off. We finally arrived in Guatemala City at 7:00 in the evening. I was so disappointed because I was sure that I would not be able to meet you until the morning.

To my wonderful surprise, my adoption agency was able to arrange for your foster mother to bring you to our hotel room that night. I'll always remember you coming into the room down a short hallway in your foster mother's arms. You were wearing a blue polo shirt, blue jeans, and the whitest baby shoes I had ever seen. You looked at me shyly, but did not want to leave the arms of your foster mother. Your foster mother fed you a bottle while we talked. Then I offered you a stuffed bear, but you had no interest. Finally, your foster mother handed you to me and she gave you a kiss on the head. Your foster mother and I hugged and said good-bye. As soon as she left, you let out a big sigh and feel asleep on my shoulder. I thought, "Wow, that was easy!"

With all the airplane mix-ups, your Great Aunt Nila and I had not eaten all day. We were starving, so we ordered some room service. The food looked great. I tried to eat with you in my arms but it just wasn't working. I thought you were sound asleep, so I laid you down on the bed. Well, huge mistake! You awoke and cried and screamed for the next three hours. I'm sure you woke up everyone in the adjoining hotel rooms. I held you and tried to soothe you, but nothing helped. You screamed and cried but did not let go of me. You clung to me. I felt so badly for you. You had just lost your beloved foster mother and were now in the arms of a very scary stranger: your forever mother. Finally you fell back asleep, and I ate my very cold dinner at midnight with you asleep in my arms. I wasn't going to put you down again; I had learned my lesson.

From your very first sigh in the hotel room to our arrival into the United States a week later, you were my Velcro baby. You clung to me with all of your might. You were attached to my hip 24/7 and spent almost every moment strapped to my chest. We visited a coffee plantation, explored Antiqua (an ancient city), were amazed by the weird foods in the open market, had lunch at an outdoor café with a view of a volcano, and saw very cool animals at the national zoo—all with you strapped to me in a blue baby carrier. You were only ten months old but you were getting heavy. So once I tried to put you in a stroller (only two feet from my reach), but you protested very loudly; you screamed and cried. I'm sure that everyone in the hotel thought I was torturing you. So I immediately picked you up and put away the stroller. Having to change your diaper was a major event. If I moved you even a few inches from my chest you would cry and scream. As soon as you were clean and dry and back in your baby carrier on my chest, you stopped crying and screaming. It was like an on and off switch. When I moved you away from me you screamed and cried and when I held you close you immediately quieted.

The biggest challenge was my need to shower each morning. Your poor Great Aunt Nila held you each morning out on the balcony of our hotel room as you cried and cried until I emerged from the bathroom. Every morning I would disappear for five minutes to take a shower, but I always returned. Each day I would hold you and reassure you that I would never leave you. On our very last day in Guatemala, you let your Great Aunt Nila hold you while I showered and you only whimpered. Yes, success! You were starting to trust that I would return and would not abandon you.

On Top of the Refrigerator
John, fostered at 4 to 5 years of age (and younger brother Jacob)

You and your little brother came to my foster home after being neglected by your birth mother. You had different birth fathers and neither of the men were part of your lives. You loved your mom very much and missed her desperately. After I met her, I, too, fell in love with her. She was a kind person who adored you. She was working two jobs and trying to care for you and your brother. She was exhausted and did not know how to care for you. She had to learn how to make you meals, how to clean your clothes, how to give you boundaries and structure, how to bathe you and brush your teeth, how to put you to bed, and how to get you to school, ready to learn every day. She told me that when Child Protective Services removed you from her home, it was a "wake-up call" and she was ready to learn; and she did learn. I was very proud of her, and six months after you came into my home, you were reunited with your birth mother.

You loved your mom and were very loyal to her. After a couple of months in my home, you were feeling safe and secure. You were starting to trust me, and you were developing a caring relationship with me. You were becoming attached to me. At the age of four, these feelings were very confusing for you. How do you love two mothers? You were struggling with your allegiance to your birth mother. You were puzzled by your emerging love for me, a person who only had only come into your life a couple months before. Your birth mother was also noticing that you were becoming close to me; she said, "He likes you better." I'm sure that she felt very hurt and threatened by our relationship. So during a weekend visit with your birth mother, she told you that you should love her and only her! I understand why your mother told you this, but it was very hurtful to you, and you returned to my home very stressed. You were conflicted, confused, bewildered, and scared. So your solution was to get rid of me. You had a plan to kill me. If I was gone, you would only love your mother and that would end your anguish and please your mother. You had a plan. You were going to take a sharp knife from the kitchen drawer and stab me while I slept. Luckily you told me your plan, and I immediately moved all of the knives (even the butter knives) out of your reach. For about a month, if I needed a knife, I would grab one off the top of the refrigerator. You and I talked. We also "wrote" children's stories (we made up stories and drew pictures) about caring for two mothers. We also talked to your birth mom and we all agreed that yes, you can care for both your birth mom and me, your temporary mom. We gave you permission to care for both of us. You evidently accepted your feelings and our relationship grew stronger and your relationship with your birth mother also gained strength.

Mom Be Back
Wu LeBin, adopted in 2015 at almost 8 years of age

You had been home for exactly one year after I adopted you from an orphanage in the People's Republic of China. Your grandmother was visiting for a week and she was caring for you for a short time so that I could take your brother to an eye doctor's appointment for an eye injury he had sustained a few days before. I typically took you everywhere I went, but you were not able to go to your brother's appointment. At almost nine years old, you had very little language, and as a result of autism and cognitive deficits, you had the social/emotional skills of a toddler. Before I left I told you I would be back and I gave you a fist bump.

For the first ten months after your adoption, you were glued to my side. You never let me out of view and wherever I went you followed. If you were able to anticipate my movement, for example going upstairs to bed, you quickly darted in front of me to make sure you weren't left behind. There were many times we collided as you tried to beat my next step. If one of your siblings or I put on shoes or a coat, you immediately ran to throw on your coat and boots. You always beat us to the car. You were petrified that we were going to leave you behind. If I had to leave you with your grandma or your aunt you would protest, scream, cry, kick, hit, pound your fist, and run after me. You were desperate and terrified that I would leave you forever. One morning I had to leave you for only a few minutes with your grandmother and you hit the dining room window so hard with your fists, your grandma thought for sure it would break. Your grandmother and aunt (the only two people I could leave you with), told me that you would always, eventually, settle down after thirty minutes of crying, kicking, and hitting. I always came back. When I returned, rather than greeting me with smiles and hugs, you would throw your body on the floor face down, cry, and kick your feet. Boy, were you mad! You were not able to verbally communicate with us. And I am assuming that you were overwhelmed and confused by your mix of emotions regarding my leaving and my return. Luckily you were obsessed with cars, trucks, and busses so you loved the school bus and gladly went to school. However, if I was late picking you up after school you would have a meltdown and I would have to pick you up off the ground and try to wipe away your tears.

A year after your adoption, and after hundreds of separations and reunions, I had to take your brother to another eye doctor's appointment. You were playing at the dining room table with Legos® when your brother and I got on our shoes and coat. You hopped up to get your coat and race to the car. I told you that you had to stay with Grandma and that I would be back. I guided you back to your Legos® on the table and gave you our habitual fist bump goodbye. You returned to your project and said "Bye." No crying, no fighting, no running after us—wow! Could it be that after a year, you finally trusted that I always come back? Two hours later, we returned. I was expecting an emotional scene. But there was no crying, no throwing yourself on the floor, no kicking, and no fussing. I greeted you and prompted you to say, "Hi, Mom." You repeated, "Hi, Mom," and continued to put together your Lego® truck. Grandma explained that you did not fuss or cry while I was gone. She told me that about thirty minutes before we got home, you were sitting at the dining room table still engrossed in constructing Lego® cars, when she heard you quietly say to yourself, "Mom be back." You finally trusted that I would be back. After a year I could finally say that you are attached.

Spikey Hair
Pearl, adopted in 2003 at 9 months of age

Your caregiver brought you into the government office where I was waiting desperately to meet you. You were nine months old on that day. You were a little girl with short, spikey dark brown hair, a round face, and a "Buddha" belly. Your caregiver handed you to me dressed in a white jumper with bright yellow socks. You did not fuss. You did not cry. You did not scream. You did not struggle against my embrace. You sat quietly in my arms. You looked around the room, but refused to look at me. Your Aunt Doreen and Great Aunt Nila who traveled with me, talked to you and made silly faces, but you were uninterested. Our adoption facilitator told all the families to feed their babies before we had to board a bus and travel to the next government office. So I fixed a bottle and you were very happy to eat. You drank the entire bottle within a couple of minutes. I cradled you in the crook of my arm and looked into your eyes; well, I tried to look into your eyes. You refused to look at me. As a matter of fact, you put your arm and hand in front of your eyes so as not to see me. For the first few days together, you always put your arm up or both arms up in front of your face whenever I fed you. It was very cute but very sad; your response to the most stressful event of your life was to avoid it. Avoid eye contact; avoid the life-changing event of adoption.

Your Aunt Doreen who came to China to meet you had short spikey hair, a round face, and yes, a little Buddha belly. Even though you are Asian and she is Caucasian, you looked just like her. You seemed to like her better than me, too. It was like the two of you were meant to be together, rather than you and me. That was how it initially felt in China. You were certainly meant to be my daughter, but you and your aunt still share a close relationship.

We spent two weeks in China. We had to go to many government offices to complete your adoption; you slept during most of the adoption proceedings. You had to get a medical exam so that you could obtain a U.S. visa. We were awake for the exam but slept there and back. We did a lot of sightseeing. You missed most of the Canton Orchid Garden, the Temple of Six Banyan Trees, and the children's park; you slept while your aunts and I enjoyed the famous sights. The other families thought that you were such an easy baby because you never cried, fussed, or screamed. You just slept. I knew that you were feeling overwhelmed and sleeping was your escape. You coped by shutting down; by freezing.

I felt like your mother the moment I met you. But I didn't feel bonded to you until many months later. I was in graduate school studying social work at the time of your adoption and I remember studying attachment in one of my classes. I intellectually understood the cycle of attachment and knew that feelings of attachment took time to develop and expecting immediate feelings of love and bonding was unrealistic. However, emotionally I was devastated. I wanted and needed to feel bonded to you. The first few months you were home, I knew you were mine, but you felt like a stranger in my house. I also wondered if you were meant to be your aunt's daughter, because you looked and acted just like her. Your initial freeze response to the stress of your adoption—avoidance of eye contact, lack of responsive smiling, no interactive communication, no laughing or squealing—made the process of attaching to you more difficult. There was no reciprocity and limited enduring connections. It took time (a few months) and repeated positive interactions between you and I before I felt attached. It was weird. I knew I was your mom and that I loved you, but it took time for me to feel bonded to you. Of course, now I cannot imagine my life without you in it. You are my daughter and I will love you forever.

My children, through foster and adoption, eventually developed an attachment with me after they trusted that I would always be there to satisfy their physical, emotional, and social needs. After millions of needs satisfied and after thousands of mother-child reunions after brief separations, my foster and adopted children learned to trust me and know that I would always be there for them no matter what. From their trust in me there emerged a loving and secure attachment. Likewise, it took thousands of positive interactions between myself and my children for me to feel confident in my parenting, to experience joy in my children, and for me to develop a loving bond with each of my children. Every child was different and every bond unique.

Listen to the Spoken and Unspoken

LESSON FOUR

Listening is probably the most important part and the most difficult part of being a parent. Listening to your child's words seems simple enough, but appreciating the intent of their communication can be tricky. What did she mean by that? What does he need me to understand? How is she feeling? What response does he need or expect? Understanding the words not spoken can be impossible. What are they thinking or wondering but never express? Silences can be more meaningful than a thousand words. Sometimes thoughts unspoken are even more important than what is said. Observing and interpreting unspoken communications can be very challenging. Our children's behaviors and non-verbal language cues typically tell us more than what a spoken word can do. But what is he trying to communicate? What does she want me to understand? Communication is the most difficult exchange for all human beings. Successful and meaningful communication between parents and children is critical to a child's well-being. What are they telling us through their words, actions, and silence?

At the Top of the Stairs
*Cole, fostered at 6 to 7 years of age (and your younger sisters
Amanda and Lisa)*

It was only four days before Christmas, when you and one of your younger sisters arrived at my foster home late one night. It was very cold outside and you walked through my front door with a spring jacket, a short sleeved shirt, pants, and ripped sneakers. The caseworker was carrying a black garbage bag that contained a couple of soiled stuffed animals and some clothes for you and your sister. I greeted you and then took your hand to guide you to your bedroom at the top of the stairs.

By the age of six, you had survived horrific abuse and neglect by your mother and stepfather. I'm sorry, life shouldn't have been that way for you. You were the target of much of your stepfather's violence and emotional torments. Your sister was his biological daughter and he was kinder to her, although still abusive. Your mother loved you, but was also victim of your stepfather's ferocity and wasn't able to protect you. She cared for you, but did not know how to take care of you. You and your sister (and your newborn baby sister who arrived soon after you did) lived with me for a year and a half. It took you a very long time to trust me and know that no one would harm you.

The caseworker found you, your sister, and your mother walking on the city streets the night you came to my home. You were cold, dirty, and hungry. It was very late and you and your sister were scared and exhausted. The first night I quickly fed you and then cuddled you and your sister in warm blankets. You both fell asleep in your new bedroom at the top of the stairs. You arrived right before the holidays, so for the first week and a half you had no school and we were able to spend time together at home. Initially, you were very quiet and cautious. You spent hours exploring the house, looking in every room, every closet, and every cabinet. Your sister clung to her well-worn stuffed dog, but you had no interest in the items sent from your mom and step-dad's house. We went shopping and you bought new clothes and a few new toys (not too many as Santa was coming in just a couple of days). You put your clothes away in your dresser and carefully placed on the shelf near your bed your toy car and a stuffed animal you had just bought.

Santa Claus must have known what a special child you are. He arrived around midnight on Christmas Eve and had brought so many gifts for you and your sisters that they didn't fit under the tree. Then as Santa continued his journey Christmas night to bless other good little boys and girls, he couldn't get you out of his thoughts. He knew that you had been a very good boy and that you had endured many things that no child should have to experience. Thus, Santa (Toys for Tots volunteers) returned five hours later and filled the front porch with more presents for you and your little sister. You had a wondrous Christmas. You smiled for the first time. You had a beautiful smile.

After a month or so, you were settled into school and felt comfortable in your new home. You felt secure in the knowledge of the mundane: those daily activities that we all take for granted ("we" meaning persons without a history of abuse, chaos, or neglect). You now knew when our family ate, where your clothes were stored and cleaned, what time the bus came for school, how to brush your teeth, who was in your foster family (mom, grandma, grandpa, auntie, the cat and the dog) and that every night after dinner, you and I did your homework. You knew that you were safe; that no one would harm you. You also began to trust me and knew that no matter what you did or said I would not leave you. With all of that figured out you had the time, energy, clarity, and security to explore more important things; you began processing your past and worrying about your future.

For the next four months, you had behaviors that expressed your extreme emotional turmoil. Almost every night, after urging you to get out of the car and come inside (which could take up to ten minutes), you would sit on the kitchen floor with your arms wrapped around your knees rocking back and forth making guttural sounds and banging your head against the cabinet doors. Nothing I did could coax you out of your trance. I couldn't reason with you, bribe you, or console you. I always stayed close and often would sit next to you in the same position as you, never saying anything (you weren't able to listen, and to be honest, I didn't know what to say anyway). Initially after about fifteen minutes you would just "snap out of it" unpredictability and then go off and play. Eventually, as I sat near you on the kitchen floor, you would slowly inch nearer to me, then you would sit next to me, then you would place your hand on my knee, then you would allow me to put my arm around your shoulder, then you would welcome an embrace, then very slowly your rocking and head-banging disappeared.

During this same time, at least once a week on the way to bed, you would stop at the top of the stairs. You would sit on the floor (carpeted rather than the hardwood of the kitchen, so it was much more comfortable) in the same fetal position with your knees tucked under your chin and your arms wrapped tightly around you. You didn't rock or make nonsensical sounds; instead you talked to me. Very calmly and unemotionally you would tell me that you did not want to live; that you were afraid to live; that you did not deserve to live; that life was too hard; and that it would be better for everyone if you were dead. You had plans to end your life. You were going to drink poison, jump off the roof, and stab yourself with a knife. I must say that you were never out of my sight. I locked the high cabinet where I kept the cleaning supplies, and I hid all the knives. You were only six years old! How is it even possible that any child's life could be so tormented that they would plan their end? I listened compassionately while trying to hide my anguish, my sadness, my fear, my anger, my disbelief, my anxiety, and my helplessness. Our time at the top of the stairs lessened over time and you slowly became a joyful and playful child. I was relieved and grateful.

Every night since your second night in my home, you and I read a bedtime story to your sister. Then I would sit on your bed and listen to your stories, your questions, your worries, and your hopes. Your silent rocking in the kitchen, your out-pouring of emotions at the top of the stairs, your words of questioning and wisdom after your bedtime story, and your unspoken intentions, were loud and clear. I can only hope that my spoken and unspoken communication with you helped you overcome your past history and prepared you to tackle your future.

Babies on the Wall
Rose, adopted in 2001 at 11 months of age

On the evening of November 3rd, you told me an interesting story. You were only four months past your third birthday. You pointed to an area on the floor and told me that was China. You told me you were going to see Chinese people and you stepped into the area and pretended to close a door behind you. You then said, "Hi, China people, hi, hi, hi." I asked if the Chinese people were nice, and you said yes. Then you said you were mad at them. I asked you why you were mad. You told me that they put their babies on top of walls and that made you mad. You continued to say that mamas, daddies, and big sisters put the babies on the wall. You yelled, "No mama and daddies; no put babies on walls." I asked what the babies did on the walls. You said that bumble bees come and get their eyes. Then you said, "Mamas, daddies, sisters, brothers come get your babies." I asked if they came to get their babies, and you said yes! I asked if you were still mad at them. You said that you were not mad anymore.

Where did this story come from? You were so young. We had always spoken positively about China and its people. We never discussed the plight of China's babies in the era of China's one child policy. Your insight is unexplainable. I listened in awe and disbelief. Could a child so young understand the complexities of the human condition in her home country?

One Little Hop
Wu LeBin, adopted in 2015 at almost 8 years of age

I had two very short videos (less than 30 seconds each) of you from China. The first had you running around a small play room and climbing into a ball pit. One of your caregivers stopped you temporarily to ask you your name and you hesitated, but then repeated your name when prompted. I assumed that you had paused because you thought what a ridiculous question to be asked: they knew your name. Now I know that you did not understand the question or know the answer. The second video was of you standing with your caregivers and eating a chocolate pudding cup. You followed your caregiver over to where they kept the snacks. On the way you walked a couple of steps and then you made a little hop. Your caregiver gave you a pudding cup and guided you, hand over hand, back to where the staff were standing. You very skillfully opened the pudding cup with your teeth and held the cup between the fingers of your deformed hand. You happily ate the pudding with the smallest spoon I have ever seen. You did not speak in this video, but no one asked you to speak. You looked into the camera and appeared interested.

Your one little hop haunted my thoughts for months. My gut was telling me that something wasn't right. But the adoption agency remained steadfast in their story that you were a healthy little boy who had a hand and arm deformity and nothing else. After asking multiple times, they did concede that you may have cognitive delays (I believed cognitive deficits) but they were adamant that you were not autistic. A staff person from the adoption agency visited you in the orphanage; she saw you so I trusted her when she told me that you were not autistic. I only had two short videos and an incomplete medical report, so I had to trust her. You were speaking to me through those two short videos and that little hop, but I didn't trust myself enough to really listen. You were telling me that you were autistic.

Our children have much to say. Listening allows us to learn about them: what they like and what they don't like, what they need and what they don't need, how they feel and why they feel that way, what they fear and what they love, and what they dream of and aspire to. Children have profound insights, silly observations, and fresh new ideas on the world that give us a new or renewed view. We just have to listen to their words, their behaviors, their non-verbal communication, and their silence.

Play and Giggle
LESSON FIVE

When I adopted my youngest son just before his eighth birthday from a Chinese orphanage, he could only say a few Mandarin phrases. His favorite was (wǒ xiǎng wán): "I want to play." I want to play are the most important words of childhood. Every child should have the opportunity to play and be joyful. Many of our foster and adopted children are deprived of play and denied joy in their lives before adoption or fostering. Whether they survived an abusive or neglectful home or lived in a sterile institution, they lacked playtime and laughter.

Many of our children need to learn how to play. We know that children learn through play, but for some of our children who were in orphanages or abusive homes, "playing" is something they need to learn how to do. My second daughter had never seen a toy prior to her adoption. Her orphanage was very clean and orderly but was devoid of any toys, music, or books. After her adoption, her aunt and I daily took her to the playroom at the hotel in China and showed her how to play with the toys. At first she was uninterested, or more likely, overwhelmed. It took time and practice, but she learned to explore and to have fun. She watched, over and over for days, as her aunt pushed the buttons and switched the levers to pop up farm animals hidden under trap doors. Finally she reached out and grabbed onto the yellow chick that popped up and we rejoiced.

As we teach our children to play and be joyful, our children teach us how to play. Parenting should be fun and give us joy. Otherwise why would anyone parent? It is hard work. Watching my children play gives me great joy, and playing with my kids lets me share in the fun. Listening to my daughter play her trumpet in the band concert often fills my eyes with happy tears. Getting beat at Chinese checkers by my daughters and their grandmother is infuriating but also tons of fun. Watching my son jump up and down with his hands in the air after bowling a strike fills me with excitement and happiness. Cheering my daughter on as she rounds third base for home gives me great delight. Racing to the finish in the game Sorry and laughing every time my playing piece gets taken off and put back to start is silly and fun. Having tickle fights, pillow fights, and pretend karate fights give us all the giggles. Our children help us find joy in parenting through play and laughter.

Parenting is fun, but it is also stressful and at times overwhelming. I'm still learning how to balance the demands and worry of parenting with the enjoyment and fulfillment of raising children. My children have taught me that laughter is a great stress reliever. I've learned that sometimes (especially when you are about to cry or scream) you just have to giggle. Giggle and you will be all right.

Giggling in the Library

Wu LeBin, adopted in 2015 at almost 8 years of age

You attend a special education program in a self-contained classroom for children with autism and/or cognitive impairments. However, you have music, physical education, art, and library with the students in the regular second-grade classroom. Your teacher sent a note home to tell me that you interrupted the class during library that day. You sat by yourself in a chair facing away from the other children and giggled—just giggled. She did not know what caused you to start, why you were continuing, or how to stop you. You giggled for fifteen minutes before you just stopped all by yourself. The librarian was understanding but would not permit you to remain in the library if you had another giggle fit. Your teacher wanted to know what to do, but I had no suggestions for her.

Quite often, you will be at the dinner table or in the car and you will disappear into your own head. You will spontaneously start giggling. We hadn't said anything witty, nothing funny had happened, and no one else was laughing. But something is hilarious in your mind! You will just sit and giggle and giggle and giggle. Just the other day, you and I were waiting in the car for your sister to get done with a game and all of a sudden I heard giggling from the back seat. It was rather ironic as we were parked in front of a comic book store, but you weren't amused by the comics. Something else was funny in your mind. For the next twenty minutes, you sat in your car seat and laughed to yourself. As suddenly as you started you stopped. Boy, I wish I knew what was so funny. I have tried to break into your trance-like state but rarely am I successful. You eventually stop, but I also don't know what brings you out of your giggle fits. I have called your name, touched your arm, and moved your body so that we are face-to-face and I have tried to get eye contact (I've never been able to do that, but I continue to try), but you just keep giggling. So now, your sisters, brother, and I just join in and giggle. Just giggle.

Shoes on the Car Roof

Lisa, fostered newborn to 18 months of age (and your older sister Amanda and older brother Cole)

A Child Protective Services caseworker called me a week before Christmas, and asked if I would foster a family with a school-aged boy, an eighteen-month-old girl, and a little girl yet to be born: that was you. Your brother and sister arrived a few days before the holiday. Your birth mother was due to give birth to you at any time. A week after the New Year, your caseworker called me at work and my secretary got me out of a meeting. The caseworker told me that I was to pick you up at the hospital right now. I did not even know you had been born! The hospital wanted to discharge you in an hour. I knew you were coming sometime, so I had a few things ready. But I didn't have any formula or diapers. So I quickly left my meeting and ran to the store to buy supplies. I arrived at the hospital and took the elevator to the maternity floor. I told the nurses I was there to take you home. I was very excited to see you, but the nurses wouldn't let me meet you until they went over the discharge instructions. All they told me was to feed you two ounces of formula every two to three hours and if you had a temperature above 100 degrees Fahrenheit to call the doctor. You were my first newborn child and I knew very little about taking care of an infant. But with this very little bit of training, the nurses entrusted you to my care. I have to admit, it was a little scary and very intimidating. You were tiny (only six pounds at birth), but beautiful. The nurses told me that you were a good eater and very quiet and content. You had a perfectly round face, petite features, and curly brown hair. Other than some minor respiratory issues, you were healthy and happy. You were a very easy baby, thank goodness. I quickly learned how to care for you and we both grew and developed.

A few months later, on a frigid and snowy winter morning, I had an important meeting at work first thing in the morning (or what I perceived as an important meeting at that time). We were rushing to get out the door. I just barely got your older brother on the bus to school. I bundled up your sister, who was eighteen months older than you. I settled you into your car seat and tucked warm blankets around you to protect you from the cold as we headed to the car. You were just three months old. You and your sister went to childcare while I worked. Your child care provider was only two blocks away, but it was too cold to walk. So I cleaned your spit-up off my suit jacket, put on my coat, and slipped on my snow boots. As your sister toddled ahead of us, I carried you, your diaper bag, my brief case, and my dress shoes to the car. I got you, your sister, and all of our stuff into the car, or so I thought. We drove around the corner to your childcare provider's home. As I unbundled you and your sister in her foyer, the childcare provider peaked outside and told me that my dress shoes were on the roof of my car. Oh my! The childcare provider and I laughed until we cried.

It had been a very stressful few months with the sudden placement of you and your siblings into my foster home, parenting three young children including you as a newborn, helping your older siblings cope with their prior traumas, and working full time. Giggling over those ridiculous shoes on my car roof was the therapy I needed. Even now, twenty years later, I always make sure that my dress shoes are inside the car before I drive off and I giggle to myself as I do it.

The Little League Parade
Pearl, adopted in 2003 at 9 months of age

It was opening day! The first opening ceremony for the newly established Crown City Little League. You were not quite six years old and playing at the Rookie level. You loved baseball and couldn't wait to play. You were wearing your Angels uniform and baseball cap that you had received the night before. I remember having to quickly sew on your Little League badge to your uniform sleeve before opening day the next morning. You have never let me forget that I put it on the wrong sleeve of your uniform; thankfully, they still let you play. You were one of two girls playing and the only child of Asian heritage in the league of over two hundred players. You didn't care who was playing as long as you could get out there and hit the ball. You were so excited.

The parking lot was overflowing with parents' cars and little boys and girls from five to thirteen years old. They were all streaming into the ballpark dressed in their new and very clean uniforms (they did not stay clean for long). Local officials and State dignitaries were there to celebrate the opening of this new Little League program on three brand new baseball fields. It was a beautiful spring day in Central New York. It was actually a warm day for the beginning of May. It was sunny with no rain in the forecast, a perfect day for baseball. The players were gathering by team on the far baseball field. The coaches were trying to keep their players in line as the excitement of the day kept building. Parents had packed the bleachers and were standing clustered around the field where the opening ceremony would commence shortly.

Here came the teams! The teams paraded around the field, passing in front of their parents, the League's founders and leaders, the local officials, and the State representative until each player kneeled with their team as they spread across the in-field line. Leading the parade of teams, holding onto the American flag was you: a girl, a Chinese child, an orphaned child, an immigrant, an athlete, a lover of the game, an intense player, a team leader, and a role model for good sportsmanship. They chose you to represent the League and lead all the players onto the field and into the promise of fun, physical well-being, skill development, team spirit, encouragement, discipline, leadership, citizenship, teamwork, victory and defeat ... and, oh yeah, baseball.

You continued to lead on and off the field in the League for the next eight years. You were the first girl to be voted onto the All League Team and the first girl to earn a position on the League's All Star Team. You earned the respect and admiration of your teammates (and their parents). When the boys were to pick a partner in a drill or a teammate for a scrimmage, you were always the first pick. It was not unusual to find parents coming to the baseball field even when their son or daughter wasn't playing; they came to watch you lead your team. It was much more than your physical talents: it was how you quietly encouraged your teammates, how you calmed your teammates in tense situations, how you respected and revered your coaches, and how you truly loved to play the game. You are now too old to play in the League, but this season you were the first girl to umpire in the League and you continue to lead by demonstrating excellence as an official.

A Twenty-Cent Napkin

Wu LeBin, adopted in 2015 at almost 8 years old, along with his siblings Marco, Pearl, and Rose, Mommy, and his aunt

Six days after I adopted you in China, your aunt and I took you, your two older sisters, and your brother to the Zoo in Guangzhou (one of the largest zoos in China). What was I thinking? I barely knew you and you did not know us at all. You understood no English and had only a couple of Chinese phrases. You did not know what to expect at a zoo or how to behave. You had never been outside of your small orphanage. In the almost eight years you had lived in the orphanage, you had never gone to a store or to a restaurant, played at a playground, or saw an animal other than a stray cat in the alley outside your orphanage. Your orphanage was on two floors of a government building in the middle of Wenzhou City. One floor had four or five small classrooms and one large room (maybe 12 x 14 feet) with a ball pit, some large balls and a couple of playground-type toys. The other floor was where all of you slept. There were two large rooms, each with beds arranged around the perimeter of the room. Your tiny bed was at the end of the room surrounded by one other small bed and about twenty larger beds. Your bed had a blue printed spread and was very low to the ground. The small entry to your orphanage was the only outdoor space you had to play. It was a cement pad in the alleyway that was about the size of a small bedroom.

Knowing all of that should have been enough for me to think twice about taking you to the zoo. Then add the challenge of autism and cognitive deficits. It was crazy, but your siblings wanted to go and it would be a once-in-a-lifetime opportunity for our family. You loved the taxi ride to the zoo. I took you and your brother in one taxi and your aunt took your sisters in another taxi. The taxi was speeding and zig-zagging through traffic. We were going much faster than we would dare drive in the United States, with cars and trucks just inches from us. I joked with your brother that we could reach out the taxi window and touch the next car. Your brother said, "Whoa, this is awesome," and loved bouncing up and down without a seat belt. You were very excited about the drive. You sat on the edge of your seat and stood up most of the ride. I was holding onto your shirt, hoping you wouldn't fly off the seat. You boys loved every minute of the ride; I on the other hand was very thankful when we arrived safely at the zoo. You kids were psyched and your aunt and I were stressed out even before we started our day at the zoo.

To enter the zoo, you first have to walk through a gift shop. We quickly made our way through the store with you in my arms (you were only the size of a four-year-old so I could carry you on my hip). You were quiet through the store, but as soon as we headed to see the first animals at the zoo, you had a major meltdown. You screamed, cried, threw your body, kicked, and hit me. I separated you from the rest of the family and sat on a bench away from as many people as I could; in China people are everywhere. You continued to throw a fit as the rest of our family continued to enjoy the beautiful zoo. To get from one animal section to the next in this zoo you had to walk through gift shops (very smart). So while we were in the second gift shop, you screamed and tugged on my arm. It was very crowded and I just wanted to escape. So we exited and then you really showed me your fury. You obviously were trying to tell me you wanted a toy. I knew that the only way we were going to get through this zoo was to get you the toy you wanted. So your aunt stayed with your sisters and brother and I took you back into the store. You took off running in the store but were obviously looking for something in particular. Sure enough, you quickly found a truck with animals. You grabbed it and ran to the check-out. We bought it and you opened it immediately. You played and played with the truck; you discarded the plastic animals that came with the toy. You did not care to see any of the animals at the zoo (live or plastic), but you enjoyed the truck. And we were able to enjoy the rest of the zoo without you screaming, crying, kicking, and hitting. Thank goodness for a five-dollar toy.

The zoo had very few signs in English and even fewer workers who could speak English. All of us were starving, so your aunt and sister went searching for food. Thirty minutes later they returned with the only things they could find: ice cream and soda for lunch! It tasted great and you and your siblings were happy to have such a fun lunch, but of course a few minutes later you were all hungry again. Luckily, we decided to continue on so that we could find the panda exhibit, and to our delight, we found a restaurant with real food. I sat with you and your brother while your aunt and sisters attempted to order. There were picture menus so they pointed to things that looked good. I'm still not sure what we ate, but it filled your tummy and you were happy with the choices.

Your aunt and I were exhausted by the time we got our real lunch. After a harrowing taxi ride, an uncontrollable meltdown with you, miles of walking in crowds of people, I was glad to be able to rest and eat for a few minutes. With four kids using chop sticks, we were making a mess and hands and faces were in need of cleaning. So your aunt and brother went to search for napkins. They were gone for ten minutes and came back empty-handed. Where were the napkins? After looking and looking for napkins they tried to ask a worker (who did not speak English) in the restaurant. After a lot of gesturing, the worker finally showed them two fingers. Yes, we need two napkins, your aunt tried to communicate. No, the worker again showed them two fingers. What did she mean? Then finally your aunt showed her money: yes, the worker wanted two yuan (about twenty cents) for a napkin. Your aunt politely (I think) declined. Two yuan for one napkin! We couldn't believe it. Your aunt and I started to giggle uncontrollably. Your sisters and brother soon joined in. We all laughed until we cried. We laughed so hard it was hard to breathe. We just couldn't help it. Luckily I found one torn tissue in my coat pocket that we all used sparingly to clean up.

Many adults, including me, forget how to play and be playful and how to laugh and be joyful. I'm convinced that children come into our lives to remind us of the importance of playing and giggling.

My kids remind me to play for just the fun of it. To get out there and play regardless of your age, your gender, your background, or your abilities. To play with purpose, while at the same time play without the purpose in mind. To giggle. Just to giggle. To laugh with intent, but without reason. To giggle until you cry, you can't breathe, and maybe you even pee a little.

Be Caring and Compassionate

LESSON SIX

When I ask prospective adoptive parents what values they hope to instill in their children, almost every adoptive parent includes compassion at the top of the list of moral principles. It is a global wish for people to be compassionate and to care for others across the planet. It is one of the crucial elements for peace and well-being. I, too, was planning to teach my children how to be caring and compassionate, but instead they taught me.

The Christmas Goat
Rose, adopted in 2001 at 11 months of age

You were only eleven months old when you were in the Nanning Children's Hospital in China being treated for life-threatening illnesses. You screamed when they sliced your finger to take blood, whimpered when they put an IV into your hand, and protested when you had to sit still during your respiratory treatments. But you never cried for yourself. I cried for you. However, when you heard another child crying in the hospital you would start crying. As you were lying there fighting for your life, you were crying for others. Your empathy and compassion for the other children were awe-inspiring. I wondered (and continue to wonder) if your caring nature was innate or learned. Were you born with a loving heart, or did your life in an orphanage teach you to be caring toward others?

Four years later, it was the first week of kindergarten and many of the children were having difficulty adjusting to school. You were doing very well and enjoyed school. Your teacher called to tell me that you were supporting the other children. She explained that you were helping a little girl who was crying on the first day of school. You sat next to her on the playground and put your arm around her and told her that she would "be okay." The next day you asked the teacher for construction paper so that you could make this little girl a card to cheer her up.

When you were ten years old, I asked you what you wanted Santa Claus to bring you for Christmas (yes, you were still a believer or pretended to believe for my benefit). You then talked about all the children who do not receive any gifts and the children around the world who don't have enough clothing or food. You wanted to give a gift to them. So without you knowing, I went to a local church that was donating money to Heifer International (an organization whose mission is to end world hunger and poverty). The money that Santa (me) donated to the church was used to purchase a goat for a family in Africa. The church wrote you a thank you letter with a picture of the children who received your gift and the two little girls in the family made you bracelets. You found the letter and bracelets in your Christmas stocking and were so tickled that Santa had blessed other children. That was the start of our family's tradition of giving. Every year, you and your siblings make a "to give" Christmas list and Santa Claus donates to the charity of your choice. Since that first Christmas, you and your siblings have shown great compassion for others. You helped Haiti's earthquake victims, built water wells in rural Ethiopian communities, supported the Red Cross, provided food for abandoned animals, gave school supplies to children with none, and families around the globe who have no food, you gave fruit trees and chickens and yes, even more goats. I am very proud of your generosity and concern for others worldwide. On your Christmas "to give" list of 2011 (you were 11 years old) you wrote: "$ to Haiti; $ for water, food to the SPCA; and a letter sent to authors, celebrities, billionaires, millionaires, trillionaires,

Obama (the President), Michelle (the First Lady), and people who have a lot of money to tell them to give lots away, like giving $100 to a charity every day."

Your spirit of caring is evident every day. You continue to cry for those who are crying.

Your Teacher Called
Marco, adopted in 2007 at 10 months of age

Your third-grade teacher called one afternoon to tell me how proud she was of you. She explained that you had become a very caring and responsible young man, rare behaviors in eight-year-old boys. She told that me that you were being a great, big brother to your newly adopted brother, Wu LeBin. You were helping your new brother adjust to school.

Your brother had lived in a Chinese orphanage for his first seven years and had only joined our family a few weeks before. He was almost eight years old but had never attended school or been outside of his small orphanage. In addition to his multiple disabilities, including autism and cognitive deficits (aka intelligential disabilities), he had no English language skills at the time. The school district had placed him into a regular kindergarten classroom with a teacher's assistant. He was overwhelmed and highly stressed by the classroom and the sensory overload of a four-hundred-student elementary school. He had no idea what was expected of him. He did not understand the schedule or rules of the classroom. He could not socially interact with his teachers or classmates. He was overstimulated by all the activities, toys, kids, noises, visual stimuli, and teachers. He did not like the food and couldn't focus in the very loud and busy cafeteria. He had no communication skills in his native language or in English. He was unprepared for any schooling and certainly did not have the capabilities needed to function in a regular classroom. He must have been overwhelmed and terrified.

Every morning, I drove you and your brother to school. You

always helped him out of the car and put his book bag on his back and handed him his lunch box. You walked him across the street and made sure he made it safely to his classroom. Multiple times every day, Wu LeBin had difficulty following the schedule of the classroom, understanding the rules of the school, meeting the expectations of his teacher, and managing the stress of the chaotic environment of a busy elementary school. In addition, he must have worried that his new mom and siblings had abandoned him in this very scary place. Due to his extreme lack of any language (his understanding was typical of an infant), I could not explain to him that he would be at this crazy new school for only a few hours a day and then would return to his new family and home every afternoon. With all of this turmoil, your brother had many meltdowns during the school day and was often out of the classroom walking the halls with his teacher's assistant.

While walking through the hallways of the school to calm down, Wu LeBin would often take his teacher's assistant to your classroom. You greeted him with, "Hi," and reassured him that you were still there for him. You told him to go back to his classroom and that you would see him later. After this quick reconnection with you, he was able to return to class. If you were out in the hall walking to a special class, like music or art, Wu LeBin always ran over to you. Each time, you helped him back to his classroom before you continued on to your special class. You were a tremendous support to your brother and a wonderful help to his teachers. At the end of the school day, you often found Wu LeBin lying on the floor in the hallway "in his own world" (your words), retreating into his own mind, oblivious to his surroundings, and ignoring the teachers who were trying to reach him. You then helped him up off the floor and escorted him onto the crowded bus. Wu LeBin was scared on the bus and often made unusual noises, like he does when he is frightened or over-stimulated. You kept him safe and helped him stay seated throughout the ride. You protected your brother from kids on the bus who were being loud or mean. You got him off the bus at the right stop and made sure he had all of his belongings. Because of you, your brother was able to get through the school day and make it safely home. Thank you for caring for your new little brother! Just like your teacher, I am very proud of you.

A Gift

Wu LeBin, adopted in 2015 at almost 8 years of age

You left your orphanage after almost eight years to meet us in a government office five hours away by car, only to be driven back to the orphanage the next morning so that we could meet your caregivers and obtain needed adoption documents in the city of your birth. I was so worried that you would be emotionally traumatized by this return visit to your orphanage. Would you be fearful that I would abandon you and leave you at the orphanage? Would you be confused by visiting but not staying at your orphanage? Would you rejoice in returning to the only home and caregivers you had ever known and be hopeful that your new brother and sisters and I would leave and allow you to stay at the orphanage? I couldn't explain to you that we were returning to your orphanage for a short visit. I wasn't able to reassure you that I wasn't going to take you back to your orphanage and leave you there. I had no idea what you were thinking or feeling. We were not able to communicate with each other due to our lack of a mutual language and the fact that you are autistic and had minimal language and cognitive skills. I had no idea how you were going to react when we pulled up to the entrance of your orphanage.

When we arrived at your orphanage, you seemed to be glad to be back. You greeted your teacher and gladly showed your siblings and I your classroom and play area. You had a very special teacher who worked with you almost every day in a small classroom that had room enough for you, your teacher, and maybe a couple more children. The room had shelves full of toys and books lining the walls and a small desk on one side of the room. Your teacher cared for you deeply. She was a young woman, maybe thirty years old.

She was tall for an Asian woman and very beautiful. She was very calm and caring towards you. Before I came into your life you called your teacher "Mama." Your teacher gave you two gifts before you left the orphanage: one package of small brown cars from a popular children's cartoon and another package of little plastic blue boats. She told us that they were your favorite toys because you could take them apart and put them back together (which you did for hours). After living in the orphanage for more than seven years, those toy boats and cars would be the only thing you would take from China other than the clothes on your back and a few snacks in your new Mickey Mouse backpack. You were leaving your caregivers, your classmates, your bunkmates, your clothes, your toys, your books, your bed, your ball pit (that you loved in the playroom) … your old life.

During our visit at the orphanage, you saw some of the other children whom you had lived with for seven years. You darted around the orphanage showing me your classroom, playroom, and bedroom (that you shared with probably fifteen other children). But you never showed us a friend or playmate. Your siblings and I saw many other children in the orphanage and a few children interacted with your sisters. One little girl came over to your sister and hugged her leg. Your sister called her the "blueberry girl" because she was so small, round, and adorable and wore a puffy blue coat. You, however, ignored the other children for the most part. The orphanage staff explained that because of your autism, you did not have any friends and mostly played by yourself or with your teacher. So to our amazement, before we had to leave the orphanage, you took one of those small plastic toy cars, which your beloved teacher had given you just moments before, out of the package. You darted away from us with the car in hand. You ran over to another little boy who was probably a year or two younger than you and you handed that toy to that little boy. You said nothing to the boy and did not show him any affection (no hug, no high five, no fist bump). The little guy accepted your gift and flashed a quick smile. You quickly ran off and joined us as we all went downstairs to have lunch with your teacher. You took a precious gift given to you and gave it to another child who had nothing: no toy, no mommy, no daddy, no sister, and no brother.

Every day, I am in awe of my children and proud of who they are. When I consider that each of my children began their life in extreme deprivation and distress, I am humbled by their contributions. I often wonder if their difficult beginnings have shaped their loving hearts. Their compassion for others and their caring spirits are inspiring. I have learned from them to be empathetic, selfless, generous, self-sacrificing, and giving. They have taught me to think of others before myself and put the needs of others ahead of my own. They are changing the world with each act of selflessness and kindness.

Be Responsive, Flexible, and Creative

LESSON SEVEN

All parenting demands that you ar responsive to your children's needs and that you are flexible and creative in your approach. Situations faced by foster and adoptive parents often require us to throw away the traditional approaches to parenting and to try new things. Following the standard rules of parenting often doesn't apply when you are caring for a child who has a history of abuse, neglect, and/or institutionalization.

For example, time-outs are a common discipline tool used with children. However, placing a child into time-out who fears abandonment, who has not yet bonded with his new parents, or who has never learned how to self-regulate his emotions, will not calm the child nor correct the behavior. Rather, it will escalate the situation and negate any intended teaching. A time-out separation from a child who is learning to trust, a child who yearns to be accepted and loved, a child who is starting to build an attachment to you, will foster mistrust, heighten their feelings of rejection, and intensify their fear of abandonment. Time-out not only assumes that a child is secure in their feelings of attachment to the family, but it also requires the child to have the ability to calm him/herself. Many children with a history of abuse, neglect, or institutionalization have never learned how to regulate their emotions. When left alone in time-out, their tantrum behaviors increase (they scream a little louder, cry more alligator tears, and throw their little bodies onto the floor). The child is never able to calm him/herself. They do not know how to calm their body and mind. Thus for our children, "time-in" is a more effective behavioral tool. Time-in has the same intent and outcome as time-out but is a non-traditional approach to discipline. Time-in removes the child from the negative situation, gives the child the opportunity to calm, restores the parent-child relationship, and then teaches the desired behavior. The difference between the two techniques is that you don't separate the child from you; rather, you remain with the child, you stay by their side, whether sitting on the bottom step or walking around the house a few times together. The child learns to remove themselves from an upsetting incident or inappropriate behavior, to gather themselves emotionally, and then to evaluate and repair their behavior (same as time-out). But more important, they learn that their parent will always be there for them and will never leave them even in their worst moments. It builds attachment and feelings of security. It also helps them identify their feelings and develop the ability to regulate and manage their emotions. This simple but profound difference in a parenting technique makes all the difference to children joining a family through adoption or foster care.

Foster and adoptive parents, even with the often disapproving eyes of grandparents and friends who have successfully used traditional parenting approaches, have to rewrite the parenting books and use individualized parenting techniques that work for their child. We often have to alter the rules and ask for others to bend the rules a little to ensure that our children's needs are being met. We need to look at parenting from the viewpoint of our children, and then figure out what they need to be successful.

A Baseball Cap for School

Cole, fostered at 6 to 7 years of age (and your younger sisters Amanda and Lisa)

I took you and your little sister shopping for clothes two days after you arrived in my foster home and only two days before Christmas. It was a busy shopping day, but you needed something to wear. You picked out shirts with trucks and cars on them and a few pairs of blue jeans. I grabbed you some socks and underwear. Then you saw a rack of baseball caps and asked politely if you could get one. If I remember right, you picked out a blue New York Yankees baseball hat. You wore it home (price tag and all).

Before you came to my foster home, you had just started school. You were a small, thin child with long, shaggy, and unkempt blonde hair. Your kindergarten teacher reported that you never completed homework and that you came to school dirty and in clothing not appropriate for the weather. Your teacher noticed that you had a round bald spot on the side of your head and discovered that you were pulling out your hair strand by strand (presumably due to stress). That is when your teacher called Child Protective Services to report your parents for abuse and neglect. Soon after, you were removed from your parents' care and came into my foster care.

At first, you willingly went to school. But after your second week back to school, you refused to board the bus for school. I was perplexed. Last week you seemed excited to go to school and every night you told me about all the fun adventures you had had at school that day. I called your teacher and she agreed that you were enjoying school and were for the first time eager to learn. I just couldn't understand what had changed in only a few days. I was driving myself crazy trying to figure out what was wrong. Was another child bullying you? Were you frustrated by the work? Did you not like your teacher? For a week you cried every morning and begged me not to send you to school. The school bus driver would arrive and you would refuse to go, so the driver would go pick up all the other children on his route and then return to our house hoping you would be ready to go to school. Every day you would finally wipe away your tears and reluctantly board the bus. You were breaking my heart, but why? I asked you many times why you did not want to go to school, but you didn't (or couldn't) answer.

Finally as the bus waited outside our door, on a Thursday morning, with tears streaming down your face and your coat pulled up over your head you told me in a quiet voice, "The school won't let me wear my baseball hat in the classroom." It all made sense now. I did not need to ask you anything else: I understood. The night before you arrived at my home, your stepfather, suspecting that you might be removed by Child Protective Services, had shaved your head so that the bald spot on your head where you had pulled out your hair was barely noticeable. For the first couple weeks of school no one noticed your bald spot but now that your hair was growing out the area with no hair was very evident. As a matter of fact, it took over a year for your hair to grow back in that spot. I quickly called your teacher to explain and she agreed to allow you to wear a hat in school. You dried your eyes, put on your New York Yankee baseball cap, and with a smile on your face you boarded the bus to school.

The Snack Bags

John, fostered at 4 to 5 years of age (and younger brother Jacob)

I remember saying often to you, "Your mother loves you, but does not know how to care for you; but she is learning now while you live with me." You came to my foster home with no bags in your hands. You arrived with only the clothes you were wearing. You had no cuddly blanket, no huggable stuffed animal, no clothes, no familiar toys or books, no comfort or feelings of safety or security. You were scared and you were hungry! Within minutes of arriving to my home, I handed you and your brother plastic baggies full of snacks.

You came to my foster home on a Friday afternoon. You were wearing dirty clothes, you had very long, broken, and dirty finger nails, and your hair had not been cut or combed for a very long time. You were very small for your age. You were four years old and your brother Jacob was two years old. You must have been terrified and unsure of what was going to happen next. You and your brother huddled together on the couch and didn't speak a word. I was uncertain of how to approach you, so I used the universal ice-breaker: food. I brought you and your brother each a bag full of graham crackers. You tentatively took my offering and got up and walked to the kitchen table to eat your treat.

I showed you around your new home. You and your brother carried your snack bags with you. Your bag was already empty, but you still brought it with you. You both liked your bedroom. The room was painted a light blue and you had matching beds with dinosaur comforters. At dinner, you gobbled down three helpings of food; I didn't think you would ever get full. After dinner, we played with matchbox cars on the carpet in the living room. You and your brother played well together and would talk with each other, but not to me. It was getting late, so I picked up a stack of books and we went into your bedroom and you listened to book after book. You were exhausted, but fought off sleep. I asked if you wanted a snack before bed; you and your brother both sheepishly said, "Yes, please." I gave you both another baggie full of snack crackers. You ate a few crackers. Then you hid the rest of your snacks in the top drawer of your dresser. Your brother put his baggie of food under his pillow. You then both crawled into your beds and quickly fell asleep.

The next morning, you both woke up early. Although we had only had a few hours to get to know each other, I had to take you shopping for clothes. You had nothing to wear. So I bathed you and washed your hair. You played in the tub with bubbles and rubber toy animals. After your bath you and your brother seemed more relaxed. With baggies full of snacks in hand, we headed off to the local JCPenney store. Before we exited the car, I explained that you were not able to bring food into the store. You understood, but your younger brother cried and cried. So I bent the rules and let you take your snack bags into the store, but they had to stay in your pockets; you agreed. I had no idea what size you boys wore, and of course you needed everything: shirts, pants, underwear, socks, pajamas, coats, mittens, hats, snow pants, and shoes. The sales associate at JCPenney was very helpful. She was very patient and kind and found everything you needed. While she was searching for clothes in your sizes, I was chasing both of you around the store. It was clear that you didn't understand the rules of behavior for shopping, and that you were not ready to listen to me. While I held onto your brother, you picked out a very special green shirt with brown trim and a truck printed on the front; that was your favorite shirt that you wore again and again. Two hours later we had success and left the store with clothes, shoes, and coats. It was exhausting and must have been hunger-producing, because as soon as we got into the car, you got into your snack bags and munched all the way home.

For the first four months of living with me, you and your brother needed the security of knowing that food would always be available and that I would never let you go hungry. I tried my best to make sure that you always had a baggie of snacks with you: in your pocket, in your book bag at school, and even tucked under your pillow every night. Even with these snack bags, I would still find food missing from the cupboard or refrigerator. I typically found food under your bed or in your dresser drawer. One day, I smelled something terrible in your room and found moldy cheese behind the bookcase. I also had a trail of ants coming into the kitchen one spring day that lead me to half a jelly sandwich behind a cupboard.

When you first arrived you ate three meals and five or six baggies-full of snacks every day. Over time the number and amount of snacks decreased. Eventually, you no longer ate the snacks, but you still wanted/needed your snack bags. After about five months, I still gave you your snack baggie, but I started to find them left on the kitchen table or under your pillow unopened. You abandoned your baggie of security a couple months before you were reunited with your birth mother. I hope that your tummy has always been full and that you have never again needed the security of snack bags.

I have bent (and sometimes broken) many rules as I have parented my foster and adopted children. My children have eaten in the living room and yes, in their bedrooms. They have enjoyed dessert before dinner. They have worn a hat in school. They have shared a family bedroom. They have gone to a movie before their homework is done. They have been picked up every time within seconds of crying. They have snuggled with their very worn-out baby blanket during an important community get-together (even though they were seven). They sat cuddled next to me after being naughty. They squatted on the floor of the concert hall and played with matchbox cars while I listened to their siblings play in the band. They took snacks to bed.

Every child is unique and has individual needs, strengths, and challenges. Every child needs to be parented differently and for our foster and adopted children, many need to be parented using non-traditional approaches with different rules and expectations.

Be Persistent and Determined

LESSON EIGHT

Nothing important in life comes easily. Just becoming a foster or adoptive parent is hard and requires persistence. Unlike biological families, foster and adoptive parents have to take parenting classes, pass a home inspection, have national child abuse and criminal history clearances, provide references, prove financial stability, have a medical evaluation, disclose life history and world view to a social worker we barely know, and answer questions about foster/adoptive parenting in the right way, in order to get approved as a foster or adoptive parent. Parents who wish to adopt from a foreign country need to obtain the approval of the United States Citizenship and Immigration Service and the officials in the country from which they are hoping to adopt. Parents who want to adopt within the United States need to gain the approval and trust of a birth family or secure the backing of a foster care caseworker. Then there is the wait: the wait for the call about a potential opportunity to meet a birth mother or to consider a child waiting for adoption. This call could happen very quickly or take many, many years. Then, as potential parents, you wait to travel to meet the child across the globe, or wait for the baby to be born, hoping that the birth mother will place her baby with you, or wait for the public welfare system to process your case and place the child into your care. Becoming a foster or adoptive parent is a lot of work. You really have to want to be a parent to endure the process. You can never give up on your dream of parenting a child. To be successful, you have to remain steadfast and be persistent in your plan.

Once your child has joined your family, persistence is even more vital. You have to be a never-tiring advocate for your child to ensure that your child receives the medical, therapeutic, and educational services they need to be successful. My children have taught me how to be persistent and determined by example and by necessity.

Grandma, I'm Practicing
Pearl, adopted in 2003 at 9 months of age

You had just turned three years old and we were visiting your grandparents. You found a yellow rubber ball, about the size of a baseball, behind a chair in their sunroom. You stood in the middle of the room and were throwing the ball up in the air and catching it, then throwing it up again and catching it, and then throwing it up again and catching it, over and over again. You probably played catch with yourself for a half hour (that is a very long time to do anything when you are three years old). Your grandmother walked into the room and asked you what you were doing. You simply said, "Practicing," and you continued to concentrate on throwing and catching that ball.

A year later, your sister, cousin, aunt, grandparents, and I went to a local miniature golf course for some fun. You went to the golf course to conquer every hole; I'm not sure how much fun you had. Luckily you did well for the first three holes. But that fourth hole was a tricky one. You had to hit the ball around a track to get it into the hole. You tried and tried and tried. And your grandfather and I tried and tried and tried to get you to move on to the next hole, but you refused. You stomped off and went back to hole number four. You hit the ball over and over and missed every time. It was a cold fall day and we were the only family at the golf course so you could continue your quest to master that hole. You got very angry with yourself; you got so mad that you cried and threw the golf club. We kept encouraging you to try the other golf holes, but you refused. You were driving us crazy; but you were focused and unrelenting. The rest of us were almost done with the eighteen holes, and you were still back at number four. You just would not give up. You finally got the ball in the hole. Thank goodness!

Your persistence continued. When you were eight years old, you wanted a rip stick (a skate board with only two center wheels) that was designed for children ten years and older. I relented and got you one for your birthday. You spent hours outside trying to ride your new board. You would hold onto the side of the house to steady yourself. You fell off the board many times. You got back on every time—well, almost every time. I do remember you storming into the house on numerous occasions with tears in your eyes and anger in your voice because you couldn't just jump on the rip stick and ride down the driveway. After a few minutes of stewing you would always wipe away your tears and collect yourself and head back outside to try again. It only took you two weeks to master the rip stick. You then proudly rode your rip stick to the park around the corner.

Your untiring determination to master all sports is legendary. You spend hours shooting, throwing, catching, and hitting. In the winter, you practice dribbling a basketball in the kitchen (often using me as a defender to spin around) and walk around the house pretending to throw a softball. When it is nice weather, you are outside doing lay-up after lay-up, stopping hundreds of grounders, swinging a bat, and bouncing a basketball between your legs and behind your back. Although you get frustrated when you can't immediately master a new skill and get very upset with yourself, you always calm yourself and rededicate yourself to the task. You never give up! Your endless practicing has paid off. You are an exceptional athlete who is respected by your coaches and teammates.

Through the Snow in Moccasins
The birth mother of Lisa, fostered newborn to 18 months of age

Your birth mother held you for the first two days of your life. Then, in tears, she had to say good-bye to you (for then) at the hospital. Two weeks earlier, your older brother, Cole, and sister, Amanda, had been removed from your mom and dad due to extreme abuse and neglect, and were brought to me for foster care. Thus, you were not allowed to go home with your mother. I arrived at the hospital to bring you to my foster home. I cared for you for the next eighteen months.

Your birth mother was granted supervised visits with you and your siblings every Thursday night in my home. A few days after you arrived in my home, your birth father was jailed for a crime against one of his neighbors and he was not given any opportunity for visitation with you or your siblings. Your birth mother had to take a bus and then walk about five blocks to get to my house. She never missed a visit. She had very little and although it was winter and there were many feet of snow on the ground and cold winds blowing, she often arrived wearing torn pants, a white t-shirt, a light jacket, and moccasin style slippers. She tried hard to play with you, your sister, and brother. She would feed you and give your siblings a snack I prepared every visit. When you were very young, you gladly let your birth mother hold you and feed you. When you were about five months old, you became very apprehensive with your birth mother. You pulled away from her and cried for me to take you. It was heartbreaking for your birth mother, but understandable (and developmentally appropriate). You knew me as your mother and your birth mother as a stranger who came once a week for two hours. For the next nine months, when your birth mother arrived at the front door you clung to me and snuggled your head into my neck, hiding your eyes from her. Your birth mother was very understanding. For months she played with you from a distance. I'm sure that she wanted so much to pick you up, cuddle, and kiss you. As you grew older, you became more comfortable with her visits and often let her hold you and read to you. Your birth mother kept trying; she never gave up.

Just a few days before you turned eighteen months old, the caseworker called and announced that the court had decided to return you and your brother and sister to your birth mother. I was to have you packed and ready to leave in the morning. After a year and half of being your mom, you were leaving forever. At first I was in shock; how was it possible that you and your brother and sister were being reunited with your birth mother without her meeting her goals, without prior unsupervised visits, without any visits with your birth mother in her home, without a plan for transition? How was it possible that a judge and law guardian who had never met you had made such a drastic decision? I was very worried for your safety. Could your mother keep you clothed, fed, safe, and happy? I was troubled by knowing that you would feel abandoned; I would disappear from your life. I was concerned about your feelings of loss and grief: I was the only home and mom you knew. I was upset knowing that you must be fearful of the unknown: where are you going and why? I was worried because I knew that you would yearn for sameness: you would have to learn a new normal. You were too young to understand, but old enough to be impacted by this abrupt change in your life. I was hoping that you trusted your birth mother enough to build a bond with her and let go of me.

I loved you and your brother and sister and would miss you desperately. I was distraught with grief. You changed my life and shaped my future as an adoptive mother. After you left, I vowed to never again say good-bye to a child; I decided to adopt and I now have four children through adoption.

First Day at a New School
Rose, adopted in 2001 at 11 months of age

We were moving to a new community so that I could pursue my career as an adoption social worker. You only had two months left of kindergarten and were doing great at school. Your first school adored you and easily accommodated your special medical needs. I debated between moving right away or waiting to move until after the school year was over. But the 1.5-hour compute one way was getting difficult and our house sold and we had to get out. You were very adaptable, and no matter where you were people immediately fell in love with you, so I wasn't too worried. You had already mastered the lessons of kindergarten: reading, counting, colors, shapes, patterns, respecting authority, cooperating, sharing, showing compassion, and playing well with others.

You did have special medical needs stemming back to your first year of life in an orphanage. Due to medical challenges, you needed more time to eat and a one-on-one aide to encourage you to eat lunch. You did have a feeding G-tube for supplemental feeding, but ate as much as you could by mouth.[8] So five weeks before we moved and you were to start at your new school, you and I met with the district and school administrators, your teacher, and the nurse to talk to them about your special medical needs. Everyone was a little nervous because you would be their first student with a feeding tube and feeding needs. But once they met you and saw your feeding tube, they felt much more comfortable. They looked forward to you coming. I then trained three classroom aides who were going to be your lunchtime feeders. The school was ready for your arrival, or so I thought.

We moved into our new home and you were ready to start in your new school the next morning. At noon the day before your first day at your new school, the school nurse called me to say that you could not come to school. The School District had decided that they could not "care for your needs" and that you would have to be home tutored. I was furious. I told the nurse that that was not acceptable and that you would be in school the next morning. I called the School District's Assistant Superintendent (the person responsible for the decision). She explained that the school district wasn't prepared to meet your feeding needs. She indicated that the classroom aides I trained did not feel able to feed you. It appeared that my training scared them. So the classroom aides complained and protested. Then instead of talking to me, the School District overreacted (even involving their lawyer) and decided that you could not come to school. They wanted to have a teacher come to our home to teach you. And if they would even consider allowing you to come to school, they wanted "professional" training in feeding you (not my training, the person who feeds you every day). I explained that I was sure that the staff from the medical center in Baltimore, Maryland where you were treated for feeding difficulties would be glad to come train the staff at great cost. Then, of course, they decided that my training was acceptable.

The Assistant Superintendent insisted that you could not come to school. I explained that you were excited to go to your new school and you had the right to an education in the least restrictive environment, which for you was a regular kindergarten classroom.[9] So I suggested that I come to school every day to feed you until the school district aides felt prepared. At first the Assistant Superintendent said that I couldn't feed you because of school liability. I thought, as your mother, how could that be a liability? I explained to her that I was your mother, your legal guardian, and I would take full responsibility for feeding you and excuse the school district from any liability. So finally, she agreed that you could come to school! I am certain that she was very frustrated by my persistent advocacy for you. Interestingly, after you first read this chapter of the book, you said to me, "I personally think she should have admired a parent who fought so passionately for their child's right to an education." My phone conversation with the Assistant Superintendent occurred while we were at your pediatrician's office; the pediatrician was outraged and ready to call his attorney to fight against the school district. I assured him that I was handling the situation and that you would be attending school starting the next morning.

You arrived at school at 8:00 a.m. You were very excited and a little nervous. Your new teacher was glad to see you. He did not have anything ready for you because he had been told that you would not be coming. The school nurse was thrilled to see you. Over the next six years at this school, you and the nurse built a very close relationship that both of you still treasure to this day.

You had a great first day. Your teacher said that you fit right in and made friends quickly. I fed you at school for the next two weeks. The classroom aides and the Assistant Superintendent observed me and they quickly discovered that feeding you was simple. The school officials held another meeting with me and the school district's physician to set a "plan," which of course I believed we had finished six weeks ago. Finally, a school aide started feeding you. She enjoyed you and agreed that feeding you was the best part of her day.

I must admit there have been many times that I have wanted to give up. The foster care and adoption process is very hard and unpredictable. Parenting children with difficult histories, special medical needs, and learning differences is challenging. Advocating for my children's medical and educational needs is frustrating and overwhelming. When I'm ready to throw in the towel, I remind myself of my children's tenacity and their determination to overcome their past and current challenges. I think about Pearl's determination to make that golf shot, or Rose's intensive focus on drawing the perfect hand, or Marco's grit when throwing a bowling ball for a strike, or Wu LeBin's never-ending dedication to making the perfect Lego® truck. If they can continue their commitment and strive for their personal achievement, so can I.

Be Forgiving
LESSON NINE

Once I calm down after my initial emotionally-charged response to my children's mistakes, I forgive. Whether they forget to shut the car door causing my car battery to die, or they break their brother's favorite toy, causing a thirty-minute meltdown, or they drop a treasured family bowl, forgiving my children for their little indiscretions is easy once I take a deep breath and put their slipups into perceptive. Even when our children make more impactful mistakes, like losing the money you gave them for a field trip, or taking a candy bar from a store without paying, or not finishing a school project, although it may take more time and consideration, as parents, we still forgive our children. By giving forgiveness, our children can learn from their mistakes. They also learn that we will support them as they take the risks they need to learn regardless of whether they fail or succeed. Giving forgiveness also reassures our children that they are loved no matter what; that our love is not contingent upon good behavior or successful decisions. As our newly adopted or foster children are attaching to us, it is vitally important that they know that we are there for them regardless of their successes or failures. In addition, by showing our children compassion, tolerance, understanding, and forgiveness, we instill in them these important values.

Asking for and accepting your child's forgiveness is much harder. I find my children are very quick to forgive me for an unfair family rule, a misspoken criticism, a missed school event, or a forgotten pickup. We just have to remember to ask and then allow ourselves to accept their forgiveness. Then we have to forgive ourselves. For-giving yourself is often the most difficult task. I have really struggled with forgiving myself for missing all the signs of my younger son's multiple disabilities. I am still having difficulty forgiving myself for dashing my older son's dream of having a brother to play with. I struggle with the fact that my new son's needs are depleting my financial resources which limits opportunities for my other children. My children have forgiven me, but I am still trying to find a way to forgive myself. A year after my younger son's adoption, I broke down while standing in my kitchen with my mother by my side (she came to stay for a week to help care for my older son after an eye injury). Through my tears I heard my mother say, "You need to forgive yourself."

Forgiving individuals, institutions, and societies who hurt chil-dren, such as abusive and neglectful birth parents, unresponsive school administrators, over-worked orphanage staff, oppressive gov-ernments (e.g., one-child policy), and biased societal expectations and restrictions (e.g., caste systems, patriarchal structures), is very difficult. Parents, school personnel, caregivers, and government offi-cials are responsible to ensure the well-being of all children. They are expected and required to "do no harm." Persons in charge should always do what is in the best interest of children. When people in authority positions harm a child or neglect to prevent the harm to a child, I must admit, I have a very hard time forgiving them. However, I have learned that the person or institution with whom I am upset is never hurt by, and experiences no ramifications from, my lack of forgiveness. I am the one who is negatively affected by my lack of forgiveness. I spend a lot of negative energy holding grudges and resentments. I lose valuable sleep and experience tremendous stress, while those who have harmed others are unaware of my distress and are unaffected by their indiscretions. Forgiveness does not mean that we excuse their actions or ignore the damage they created. Rather, it restores the energy we need to advocate for our children and fight for the reform needed to prevent further harm.

Great Grandma's Mixing Bowls
Rose, adopted in 2001 at 11 months of age

When you were five years old, you, your sister, and I were making chocolate chip cookies using your great-grandmother's mixing bowl. I stepped away for just a moment. You decided to try to stir the very thick batter and knocked the bowl off the table onto the kitchen's tiled floor. I heard a loud crash and turned to find the batter spattered on the floor and Great-grandma's bowl shattered into thousands of shards of glass. You and your sister were still perched on your chairs, looking at me with shock and horror in your eyes. I screamed, "Nobody move." I did not want you or your sister to get cut by the glass. While I cleaned up the mess, I yelled at you for being careless and told you that you had broken a hundred-year-old bowl that I used to make dinner rolls for Thanksgiving every year with my grandmother, your great-grandmother. You were devastated and cried and said, "I'm sorry," over and over and over again. I eventually calmed down and came to the realization that it was just a bowl. We can make cookies in another bowl and the memory of making rolls with my grandmother was still a wonderful memory even without the bowl. I accepted your apology and told you over and over and over again, "It's all right; it was an accident; it's okay." Then I had to ask for your forgiveness for my overreaction to the broken bowl and ruined cookie batter. I was so sorry for hurting you. You easily forgave me; it took me much more time for me to forgive myself for overreacting.

Ten years later, you were softening butter in the microwave above the stovetop to make the crumble topping for apple crisp (your favorite dessert). Your great-grandmother had four nesting mixing bowls that were orange colored with a print of wheat on the side. The largest bowl in the set was the one that was broken while making cookies many years ago. Now you were using the smallest bowl in the set. I heard the microwave timer ding and then I heard a very loud crash. Your fingers were slippery from putting the butter into the bowl and when you picked up the bowl it simply slipped out of your fingers and landed on the glass stove top. I turned around and found butter spattered all over the burners and stove top controls. The little bowl was splintered into thousands of tiny pieces, shattered on the glass stove top, the counter, and the floor. I still can't believe the glass stove top did not break. You were unharmed, at least physically. You were once again devastated. You said, "I'm sorry," over and over and over again. As I cleaned up the mess I took a deep breath and told you that it was okay. It was just a bowl and a little butter. I tried to joke with you about two bowls down, two to go. You didn't think it was very funny at the time. You eventually did forgive yourself. We still have two of your great-grandmother's mixing bowls that we use to make chocolate chip cookies, apple crisp, and many other tasty treats.

Two Years of Terror
Cole, fostered at 6 to 7 years of age (and his two younger sisters, Amanda and Lisa)

Your stepfather hurt you. I'm so sorry that you experienced such cruelty. The man who was to love you, protect you, and care for you was harsh and abusive. You lived with your stepfather for two years before you arrived in my foster home; your father was a very scary man. I was frightened by him as an adult, so I can't imagine being a five-year-old and two-year-old in his home. He beat you, denied you food, yelled at you, threatened to kill you, threw things at you, beat your mother in front of you, and exposed you to inappropriate images at a very early age. Even after serving as a foster parent for many years, I have never understood how any parent could harm their child. There is no excuse for a parent to hurt their child physically, emotionally, or sexually. I may have been able to understand his behavior if he had been abused as a child, or if he was under the influence of drugs, of if he was an alcoholic, or if he had a brain injury, or if he had mental health difficulties. These factors may have explained his behavior, but would still not have excused his abusive behavior. I was furious at your stepfather for hurting you. Your stepfather did not deserve my forgiveness; I had a very difficult time forgiving him. But once I realized that my lack of forgiveness was only hurting me, because your stepfather did not know nor did he care if I gave him forgiveness, I allowed myself to forgive. I have always wondered if you have forgiven your stepfather.

On the Edge of the Bathtub
Wu LeBin, adopted in 2015 at almost 8 years of age

It was midnight, only eight hours before our interview at the U.S. Embassy in Guangzhou, China, to hopefully obtain a U.S. visa so that we could go home and you would be permitted to enter the United States and become a U.S. Citizen.

Two days earlier, you had had a medical exam, as required by the United States Citizenship and Immigration Service, to issue you a U.S. visa. That morning you woke up limping. Now what!? The day before I had had to carry you through an airport so we could fly from your Province to Guangzhou, China. You kicked and screamed for hours in the airport. Luckily, as soon as we got on the plane you settled down and enjoyed the flight. After landing, we had to walk miles through the airport to get to our taxi that was to take us to our new hotel in Guangzhou. By the time we arrived at the medical clinic the next morning, you had trouble putting weight on your right leg. Now what was wrong? Typically the medical evaluation needed for the application for a U.S. visa is a quick and cursory exam. Usually the doctor listens to your heart and lungs, checks your hearing and vision and tests for TB. Most families are in and out of the medical clinic in ten minutes. We were there for more than an hour. The first doctor examined you, re-examined you, and then brought in a second doctor to examine you. The doctors were perplexed. They tried to get you to follow simple directions, but you were not able to comply. They looked, looked, and looked again at the dimple at the bottom of your spine. They talked with each other in Mandarin and examined you again and again. I, of course, had no idea what they were talking about but I had my suspicions: autism, spina bifida occulta, cognitive deficits, hip problems, language delays, and so on. Finally, one of the doctors sat down and told me in broken English that you, Wu LeBin, had many medical and developmental concerns, but he was unsure of the extent of the problems. He confirmed that you had a hand and arm deformity (of course), but he was also concerned that you might have hip deformities, spina bifida, and autism. I watched him write these possible diagnoses on the medical report that would be part of your application for a U.S. visa that would be submitted to the U.S. Embassy for consideration for your immigration. Of course, I was not approved to adopt a child with multiple disabilities and was in a panic that the U.S. Embassy official would not permit your adoption and not issue you a U.S. visa.

I tried and tried and tried to reach my adoption caseworker in the United States. No one from the adoption agency had contacted us during our first ten days together in China. The night before our interview at the U.S. Embassy I became desperate and called the caseworker via Skype at 7:00 a.m., 7:15 a.m., 7:30 a.m., 7:45 a.m. her time (which was 10:00 to 10:45 p.m. in China) hoping she was an earlier riser. Finally at midnight my time (9:00 a.m. in the West Coast in the United States) the caseworker called me on Skype. You and your siblings were sleeping so I snuck into the hotel bathroom and sat on the edge of the bathtub. I calmly (or at least I tried to be calm) explained to her that yes, you had a hand and arm deformity but you are also autistic, cognitively impaired, and may have spina bifida and hip deformities. The caseworker said that the social worker who visited you in the orphanage months ago who told me that you were not autistic, even when I specifically asked about autism spectrum behaviors, "had missed it" when she observed you in the orphanage. How had she missed it? It took me less than one minute to recognize that you were autistic. I also told the caseworker, on Skype, that three months before I traveled to adopt you, another caseworker at the agency had insisted that I sign a commitment letter guaranteeing your adoption, even though I questioned your behaviors. Before I signed the papers, I questioned her regarding behaviors I saw in your video and read in your paperwork. She discounted my concerns and told me that you were not autistic. She told me that I needed to sign the commitment letter immediately so that she could get it into the overnight mail within the next thirty minutes. The caseworker on the Skype call also told me that the first caseworker I worked with when I originally agreed to adopt you ten months before (and who no longer worked for the agency), "sometimes presented children in a positive light and downplayed their needs so that every child could have a family." So three caseworkers were less than truthful about your medical and developmental needs. I couldn't believe what she was saying to me.

Then, I mentioned to this caseworker that you have a dimple on the base of your spine. She explained that it was probably related to spina bifida occulta. She then shared a story of another child who had the same condition and because her parents delayed her medical assessment, she is now in a wheelchair because her spinal cord was tethered.[10] That was the last thing I needed to hear. I wasn't approved to adopt a child with your multiple special needs; would the U.S. Embassy officer allow me bring you home? I was approved to adopt a child with limb differences, cleft lip and/or palate, visual impairments, or hearing loss. I was not approved to adopt a child with spina bifida or autism or cognitive and language deficits, all of which you had. Your needs far exceeded my home study and Citizenship and Immigration Service approvals. Yes, you had a limb difference but you were also a child with autism who had the capabilities of a toddler, and now may be faced with using a wheelchair in the future (and coming home to a house that is not wheelchair accessible). I was terrified. Would the U.S. Embassy issue you a visa? I really didn't know. The caseworker was hopeful because the home study stated that I was approved to adopt a child "including but not limited to a child with an arm deformity" and that all of your additional conditions would be covered by "but not limited to." She instructed me to only answer the U.S.Embassy Official with yes and no and to not disclose that you had autism, spina bifida, or cognitive disabilities.

After talking with the agency's caseworker via Skype for a few minutes regarding your unexpected needs, she told me that I could return you to the orphanage. She said, "It's a nice orphanage." I didn't know what to say. I have to admit I was struggling to accept you as my son. I had spent hours crying and talking with your aunt trying to figure out how I could parent you and my other children as a single woman. I did not know how to parent an autistic child, or a child with spina bifida occulta, or a child with limited cognitive skills, or a child with many additional unknowns. How was I going to juggle your very demanding challenges with the needs of my other children? You would require lifelong care; how could I ask your brother and sisters to be responsible for your future after I am gone? How was I going to connect with a child who didn't understand human connections? How was I going to work full time and care for you and your siblings? I felt trapped by China and my adoption agency. But it never occurred to me to return you to your orphanage. Your orphanage was nice? It had no heat. When we visited your orphanage, it was only 50 degrees and we wore our winter coats for our entire visit and I was frozen to the core. Your orphanage had no outdoor play space. You had a concrete pad about the size of a small bedroom outside the entrance of your orphanage building where you could "play." The orphanage had one small bathroom for all the children. You slept in one room with about forty beds lining the four walls. You had one small playroom with a ball pit and a few other toys. You had one little classroom that had room for three or four students and a teacher and a few toys and books. You did have a wonderful teacher, but no family. I told your aunt who was traveling with me that it would be inhumane to return you to your orphanage. I couldn't do it! How could they even suggest it? So how was I going to make it work for you and our family? That is a question I still work through every day.

If the U.S. Embassy refused your U.S. visa, I would have to stay in the country with you for many more weeks while my social worker back in the United States amended my approval to include your multiple diagnoses. And then the U.S. Citizenship and Immigration Services would need to issue an amended approval before I could reapply for your U.S. visa. I would have to send your siblings home with your aunt while you and I stayed in China. I couldn't bear the thought of being separated from your siblings for an unlimited time. I didn't know how I would manage taking care of you by myself in an unfamiliar country without knowing any of the language. I definitely knew I couldn't afford to stay in China for much longer.

Our adoption facilitator in China got us to the U.S. Embassy very early in the morning and we were first in line. You had a very difficult time waiting in line outside of the Embassy. I had to hold you for the majority of the time because you were unable to stand with the family. You wiggled and cried and made noises and tried to run, and bothered other people in line at the Embassy. It was a very long thirty-minute wait to enter the Embassy. Finally, we were in and through security. We walked upstairs and were issued a case number. Luckily, the Embassy had a few toys and a playhouse to occupy children while we waited for their visa interview. You played in the small house and ran around the waiting area. There were only two other families waiting, one with a young child and one with a teenage son. We were the first family called for the visa interview. You did not want to leave the playhouse, but the U.S. Embassy officer had to see you. I picked you up and carried you to the window where the officer greeted us. You were unresponsive to his attempts to engage you. The officer was a very kind gentleman. He verified our identities and asked if I had completed your adoption. He then looked through the visa application documents, including your medical report and my home study report. I was very nervous and certain he was not going to allow you to have a visa. My home study report did not approve me to adopt a child with the medical conditions that were recorded on your visa medical report. The officer asked if I was aware that you have a hand and arm deformity, and I said, "Yes." He asked if I knew of any other diagnosis. I said, "No." Although of course I knew you had multiple disabilities, you only had one official diagnosis: radial dysplasia (your arm and hand deformity). He again read the medical report and asked if I was aware that the doctor indicated that you have hip deformities. I explained that the doctor told me that you may have hip problems but he was not sure. The officer and I were then silent as he again reviewed the medical report. He asked if I knew about any other disabilities. Of course I knew that the visa medical report he was reading stated autism and spina bifida. We were both silent; the officer must have seen the desperation in my eyes. He then suddenly announced that all was fine and that you would be issued a visa that could be picked up the next day after 3 p.m. I quickly turned away from the officer with you in my arms and with tears streaming down my cheeks. Your siblings wanted to know what was wrong. Your aunt reassured them that everything was fine and she quickly ushered us out of the U.S. Embassy. The adoption facilitator was also very worried that you wouldn't be issued a visa. When we found her outside the Embassy on the street corner she was very relieved to know that the officer had agreed to issue you a visa. I am very grateful for the kindness of the U.S. Embassy official.

It is very hard to forgive when you have never been asked for forgiveness. No one, not our original adoption caseworker who downplayed your needs, the second caseworker who seemed unfamiliar with your needs, the social worker who visited you in the orphanage and told me that you were not autistic, the person who told me to sign the adoption commitment papers after assuring me that you were not autistic, nor the adoption agency's director has ever said to me, "I'm sorry." The social worker who visited you in the orphanage before your adoption sent me an e-mail that said, "I am truly sorry for the pain and frustration that you are going through," but she never said she was sorry for misrepresenting your needs to me. As a matter of fact, after she empathized with my feelings she wrote many paragraphs justifying how she "missed it," how she did not recognize your multiple challenges. Another new caseworker for the adoption agency sent me a note acknowledging that you have more needs than anticipated and stated that "sometimes this happens." Their comments just made it even harder to forgive them. I still have days during which I cannot forgive. I know that none of these adoption workers are ever awake all night anguishing over what happened or worrying every moment about how you will be cared for through your lifetime. Most days I just don't have the energy to refuse to give my forgiveness.

A Letter to the Board
Wu LeBin, adopted in 2015 at almost 8 years of age

Soon after we arrived home from China, we were faced with yet another challenge. Getting proper education and therapeutic services from your school district proved to be very difficult. I expected that you would be a healthy child with an arm and hand deformity who may have minor developmental delays due to your life in an orphanage in China. Prior to my travel to adopt you, I met with the school and we discussed your need for English as a Second Language instruction and placement in a lower grade due to your anticipated delays. We had a plan. Within the first minute of meeting you in China, I knew our school plans wouldn't work. I e-mailed the school's principal while still in China to let him know that you had multiple disabilities including autism and severe intellectual deficits. I explained that we would need to adjust our school plans.

After we arrived home and you had had a couple of weeks to settle in, you started to go to school. The school district provided you with a one-on-one classroom aide and placed you into a regular kindergarten classroom. You were not able to participate in the classroom instruction, you did not know how to interact with your classmates, and you were so stressed by the over-stimulation and social demands that you were physically sick: you threw up in the classroom the morning of your third day of school.

On your very first day at school I requested a special education evaluation through the Committee on Special Education.[11] The school district administrator assured me that your evaluation was a priority and would be completed immediately. Well, seventy-nine days later I had a very incomplete and inadequate evaluation (federal law requires an evaluation to be completed within sixty days of the initial permission from the parent). The day after I received the written report, your Committee on Special Education meeting was scheduled with the special education administrator, classroom teacher, English as a Second Language instructor, a language translator, and multiple therapists. Each professional explained their assessment of your skills and each person with the exception of your classroom teacher and English teacher, stated that the results of their evaluation were inconclusive because you were still learning English and that you were still assimilating to our culture. There was a language translator at all of your evaluations. The translator was present at the committee meeting and stated that you had minimal language skills in your native language of Mandarin (language skills of a toddler). We were stuck in a senseless circular debate. Your autism extremely limits your language skills in both Mandarin and English, but the school administrator was requiring that you learn English so that the school district could diagnosis you with autism. Limited language skills is one of the most significant disabilities for a person with autism. The Committee on Special Education also ignored your pediatrician's diagnoses of autism, radial dysplasia, spina bifida occulta, and language and cognitive impairments. You are a child with multiple disabilities as documented by the pediatrician. Your teacher of English and your classroom teacher explained that you have exceptional needs and tried their best to advocate for you to receive special education services. The teacher of English was reprimanded during the meeting and your classroom teacher was scolded after the meeting by the school administrator for speaking up on your behalf. Without full agreement and with my very strong objection, the special education administrator announced, "At this time, no decision can be made regarding your eligibility for special education classification." I was outraged.

The special education administrator announced that the Committee on Special Education would reconsider your needs in eight months. That would mean you would not receive special education and therapeutic services for twelve months. That was unacceptable. It was the end of the school year, so I asked the Committee on Special Education to be reconvened as soon as school began in September. It would mean you would not get any services over the summer and you would remain in an inappropriate classroom placement for a few more months. The actions of the school district were inappropriate and inexcusable. I wrote a letter of complaint to the School Board.

The Special Education Committee meeting in September was much more productive and appropriate. I brought with me the reports of nine medical and psychological experts who all confirmed your multiple disabilities. Your pediatrician attended the meeting via a conference call. I brought a parent of a child with autism with me to the meeting. The same teachers, administrators, and therapists attended the meeting. The special education administrator was much more cooperative and the committee very quickly classified you with special educational needs and recommended an appropriate classroom placement and a variety of needed therapies. Two weeks later, more than ten months after arriving home from a Chinese orphanage, your educational needs were starting to be addressed.

I was furious with the teachers and therapists who were unwilling to stand up to the school district and advocate for your special needs. Although I was displeased with their lack of assertion, I was able to forgive their inaction, particularly as I watched them being intimidated by the administrator. The school district administrator was much more difficult to forgive. She denied you the right to needed services for almost a year. As a school administrator she should have ensured that your education needs were met; but instead, she blocked you from getting the services you needed. I have forgiven her and I hope she has learned to be more respectful and responsive to all student needs.

Forgiving your children, yourself, and others for tiny and insignificant blunders, for life-altering errors, and for life-threatening mistakes is difficult but necessary. Children with a history of abuse, neglect, or institutionalization need to know that their adoptive parents will stand by them no matter what. Forgiving your children gives them feelings of security and assures them of your unconditional love and support. It also allows them to take risks and learn about themselves, their family, and their world. Modeling forgiveness for your children instills in them the values of caring, understanding, compassion, tolerance, and advocacy. Forgiving yourself and others allows you to recognize the wrong and empowers you to make change through activism. Shedding the weight of resentment, anger, and bitterness will give you the drive you need to prevent future wrongs.

Remember What is Important
LESSON TEN

What seems like the simplest lesson can be one of the most difficult lessons to remember: your children are more important than anything else. We all get caught up in the busy nature of our lives. Our jobs have deadlines, emergencies (or perceived emergencies), inflexible schedules, demanding customers/clients, and unforgiving bosses. Our homes always need to be cleaned, or painted, or repaired. There is laundry to wash, dishes to clean, and dinners to make. We have family obligations and friendship wishes. We are faced with many demands and limited time.

As a matter of fact, my son has tried several ways to get my attention tonight while I'm trying to finish writing this book; so I now take a break to play a game of marbles with Marco. I'm back …. Marco beat me. Sometimes we need to take just a short break and remember to place our kids first in our lives.

The Fallen Tree
Marco, adopted in 2007 at 10 months of age

Our backyard is lined with four large and very old pine trees and many smaller deciduous trees. Although the pine needles are hard to manage and raking leaves is a pain, the trees provide wonderful shade, a home for many birds, a noise barrier against our neighbors, and most important, a great place to play, climb, and hide. One of the four pine trees was larger and probably older than the rest. It reached into the sky for about a hundred feet and its trunk was just over twelve feet around and measured three and a half feet in diameter.

It was the middle of summer and I had just arrived home from taking your newly adopted little brother to medical appointments with a cardiologist and geneticist at a children's hospital two hours away by car. The cardiologist gave me upsetting news about a potentially life-threatening heart condition your brother has, and the geneticist was intrigued by your brother but had no way to explain your brother's multiple disabilities. It had been a very emotional and exhausting day and I just wanted to come home to relax and decompress. It was a hot and humid day and you were desperate to go swimming. I needed to make dinner, wash the dirty laundry, pick up the house, finish some reports for work, and of course take care of you, your sisters, and your recently adopted brother (who I was still trying to figure out). You were unrelenting, you wanted to go to the pool! It had stormed earlier that day, but for now it was sunny and calm outside. So, I begrudgingly gave in and said okay to swimming. You rushed off to get your swimming suit, find your goggles, and grab a towel. I helped your brother get ready. I must admit I was not very happy about having to take you and your brother swimming. I really wanted to stay home and rest from the day and maybe accomplish a few household chores. Your sisters did not want to swim, so as teenagers, they decided to stay home. You, your brother, and I hopped into the car and headed to the community pool just a few minutes from our house.

We were only two blocks from the house when a storm came out of nowhere. Rain poured down, lighting struck, thunder clapped, and the wind blew hard. The storm lasted less than ten minutes. The sun returned immediately and it was again a beautiful and calm day. The aftermath of the storm was evident everywhere. There were puddles of water in the streets, leaves blown across yards, and tree branches strewn across the roadways. But you were adamant that the pool would open after the storm had passed and insisted that I continue on to the community park. Of course, when we arrived, the pool had closed due to the storm. You were devastated and threw a little tantrum. I have to confess, I was relieved to see the pool closed; now we could go home. After you calmed down, you agreed that a movie rented from the video store down the street would make everything all right. You and your brother picked out two movies: *Power Rangers* (your brother's favorite) and your choice, *Scooby Doo: Monsters Unleased*. Then we headed home. We arrived back into our driveway less than thirty minutes after we had left for the pool.

I pulled into the driveway but was stopped short. In front of us lay our oldest and largest pine tree. The tree was snapped off eight feet up from the base of the trunk. The tree filled most of our back-yard and its branches were now springing up from the ground and into the air more than twenty feet. Our mangled basketball pole and hoop were buried under the huge tree. The tree fell directly onto our neighbor's fence and destroyed every inch (it was a very old fence and they were hoping to replace it soon; just not this soon). As the tree fell it brushed up against our house and dented a gutter and smeared pine sap on our newly painted house. It was truly a miracle that the tree did not land in our kitchen or on top of our neighbor's house. Somehow the tree dropped directly down our driveway and landed between our house and the neighbor's house, which are only separated by about eight feet. The tree fell where our car had been parked only thirty minutes before.

I jumped out of the car, climbed over the many tree branches and ran into the house, desperate to find your sisters safe. They were both watching a movie in the living room which is on the opposite corner of the house from where the tree fell. You told them that our backyard was full of a tree that was toppled by the storm. They couldn't believe it. They told us that they had heard a loud sound but thought it was just noise from the storm. You and your sisters came running and were in awe of the sight of our beloved tree filling the backyard. All the neighbors quickly came over to make sure everyone was all right and to give me information about tree services that would come and clean up the mess. The mess did not matter, the basketball hoop could be replaced, the fence would be rebuilt, the gutter could be fixed, and I would repaint the house. All that mattered was that you, your sisters, and your little brother were okay.

As we reflected on the events of that day, we all agreed that your demand for my attention and your insistence on going to the pool saved us. If I had not given in to you, the car would have been demolished by the tree as it fell into the driveway. If we had been delayed even for a few minutes, we would have been buckled into the car when the tree fell and we would have been crushed. If the tree fell a few inches closer to the house, we would have had pine branches in our kitchen. If your sisters were outside playing they would have certainly been buried under the weight of the tree. It was all too much to believe!

Every day as I walk out into our backyard, I look into the empty space where our magnificent old pine tree used to stand, and I am reminded to remember what is important. To treasure the safety of my children and the gift of each of their lives. To give my attention to each of my children, regardless of my needs or tasks that are waiting to get done. To accept the challenges that lay ahead (your brother's medical and developmental needs) and move forward (go to the pool anyway). To appreciate the miracles that occur every day, including the gentle falling of a tree.

Eight Weeks Away

Rose, adopted in 2001 at 11 months of age

Ten years ago, I was working full time, attending graduate school, interning at an adoption agency, and parenting you (four years old) and your little sister (two years old). It was a very busy time. I had many commitments, but none more important than you. You were struggling and needed medical treatment as soon as possible.

From the moment you were put in my arms outside the elevators in the Chinese hotel, you refused to eat. In the first three years after your adoption, I tried everything. I tried all types of foods, all consistencies of food (pureed, semi-solid, solid), all temperatures, all textures, and nothing interested you. I did not care what you ate, as long as it had calories. But you did not like candy or cookies and you refused to eat at fast foods restaurants. One of your medical specialists told me to take you to McDonalds every day; I told him I could take you but you would never eat there. You never put anything into your mouth and certainly not food. When a spoon came near, you closed your lips tight and turned your head. When you finally accepted food, you pocketed it in your cheek for hours. On the few occasions when you did eat something, I cheered each time you took a bite. You looked at me with curiosity, but did not care for my clapping. It was exasperating! I did not know how to help you. Parents of young children are responsible for feeding their kids, and I was failing.

Why were you refusing to eat? No one had the answer. You were seen by many pediatricians, all of whom told me that you would eat when you got hungry enough. Well you never got hungry; you were not going to eat. We learned many years later that you do not experience the feeling of hunger, presumably because you were severely underfed (starved) at the orphanage which caused your brain to "turn off" your biological hunger trigger. Anyway, I sought out experts in feeding and gastrointestinal problems, only to be given partial answers and misplaced advice about how to get you to eat. You were examined by multiple medical specialists and were seen by a feeding therapist. But regardless of what they tried (and what I tried based on their expert advice), you continued to get through the day eating as little as possible. You were tiny and not getting any bigger. It was scary. Finally, we ran out of options and you were given a feeding tube through which I fed you formula overnight while you slept. You finally started to gain weight!

You were adding pounds for the first time, but you still would not eat. Why? I researched feeding intervention clinics and found only two in the Eastern part of the United States. I was hesitant, but knew that I had to act. It was a nine-month wait to get into either program. I hoped you could make it that long. You were getting worse and starting to lose weight, so I desperately called the feeding clinic and begged for an earlier admission. To my surprise they told me that a family had cancelled and they could accept you starting the following week. Your participation in the program would require me to be away from family, from work, from graduate school, and from my internship for eight weeks. The clinic was eight hours away by car and you and I would be staying at the local Ronald McDonald House during your treatment.

I had only a few days to rearrange my life. I had work responsibilities with multi-million-dollar deadlines. For my internship, I had clients relying on me to provide services required for their adoptions. I had school projects due that were required to complete my degree. I had your little sister to care for. I had so many demands, but nothing was more important than your life. My employer was compassionate and understanding and without any hesitancy granted me medical leave. My clients were understanding and were transferred to other social workers. With only four weeks left in the semester, my graduate school allowed to me hand in work early and complete the remaining learning through independent study. Your grandparents quickly volunteered to care for your little sister. In just a few days, all of my commitments were handled and I was ready to commit myself one hundred percent to your treatment. You were important; nothing else was more important than you.

You participated in daily treatment for eight weeks at the feeding clinic. You made some progress, but stilled struggled with eating and continued to need the feeding tube. Although this feeding clinic was at a prestigious medical facility and was considered one of the best programs in the country, they presumed that your feeding issues were behavioral and dismissed any possible medical cause. Their behavioral techniques resulted in only minor improvements because they ignored any possible medical reasons for your behavior. After completing this feeding program with very few tangible results, I continued my quest to find answers. I found a new pediatrician who referred us to a gastro-intestinal (GI) specialist only a couple hours from home. The GI specialist quickly diagnosed you with four significant medical conditions that made eating difficult and painful. Finally some answers! I was very relieved, but also devastated, knowing that I had forced you to eat when you were in pain; I'm sorry you went through that. With medical treatment and continued encouragement to eat, you have made tremendous strides. You still rely on supplemental feedings through your feeding tube to maintain your weight, but you are now eating! I'm very proud of you.

13.7 Seconds
Pearl, adopted in 2003 at 9 months of age

With 13.7 seconds left on the clock, your eighth grade basketball team was down by one point. Your team had come from behind with a chance to win in the last few seconds. Your coach put you in the game knowing you are quick and aggressive, and your job was to steal the ball and get a score. The other team had the ball for the inbound pass. Your team was using a full-court press against your opponent. The ball was inbounded and the second pass was to mid-court where you were waiting. You picked off the pass and got the ball with 9.6 seconds to go. You threw the basketball down the court to the waiting hands of your teammate and unfortunately also a little too close to the hands of the other team. The two opposing girls bobbled the ball and the ball bounced into the hands of one of your teammates. Your teammate threw up a shot, but it was a miss. Your team lost a hard-fought game by one point. You are very competitive. You were devastated and blamed yourself for throwing away the ball and losing the game.

I knew you were upset after the game. You rode the bus home with your teammates, and I was hoping you would calm down and collect yourself on the ride home; but that was not the case. As soon as you got off the bus and into our car, I could see that you were not calm and certainly not collected. You were mad at yourself, your teammates, and your coaches; you seemed angry with the world (and maybe even the universe). You ranted and beat yourself up for more than thirty minutes. I tried to teach you a few basketball strategies for the next game; I'm not sure that you were open to hearing about them right then. So off to the shower. You seemed to feel better after a shower and a late dinner.

Later that night, you came to my bedroom and sat on the edge of my bed. It was my turn to listen and learn from you. You told me that it was unimaginable to be such a small part of the ginormous universe. And that your problems were so tiny compared to all the much more important problems of the world and universe. Your last-second mistake in the basketball game may have been temporarily important to you, but was insignificant in light of the magnitude of the world's problems.

I have so many things that need to be done. There is always a pile of dirty clothes in the bathroom, our kitchen sink is often full of soaking dishes, the garage or house or interior needs to be painted, reports at work need to be finished, my taxes are not yet filed, and the list goes on and on. I appreciate that these things need to get done, but talking to Rose about the semi-formal dance, or hitting grounders to Pearl as she hones her softball skills, or encouraging Marco to bowl with patience, or throwing the ball to Wu LeBin as he tries his best to hit the ball with a bat are more important uses of my time. The dishes will eventually get washed and the clothes will get folded, but I may never again get the chance to listen to Rose play the piano, or watch Pearl shoot a foul shot, or listen to Marco giggle over a Uno card game, or watch Wu LeBin transform a car into a robot.

I put together a photo album for my parents for their 50th wedding anniversary that chronicled their life. There were no pictures of Mom doing the laundry or Dad mowing the lawn. I don't even remember if the kitchen floor was always/never mopped or if the toys were put away neatly, and it was not important! In the more than one hundred pages of pictures, there were only two pages depicting the careers of my parents (a teacher and a business owner). Yes, their work was important and they contributed to the betterment of their community through their work; however, it never took priority over their children. I remember feeling loved, supported, and encouraged by my parents. I don't remember if my parents scoured the toilet every day or if they met all their work deadlines, or if they cooked nutritious meals every day, or if they kept the car clean, or if they pulled all the weeds in the garden. The picture book, spanning fifty years, reflected our most important memories as a family: I remember silliness and laughter, major life accomplishments (graduations, weddings), quiet times at home, playing on the swing set in the backyard, quarrelling with my four siblings, attending community events, and seeing my parents in the stands of every sports game. As you reflect on the past, you realize what is important for today: your family.

Your Child is their Own Expert
LESSON ELEVEN

As parents, we are supposed to be the experts on our children. We should know them better than anyone else. I think I know my kids pretty well, but I will never truly know them. I can observe their behaviors, listen to them express their thoughts, explore their emotions, track their growth and development, review their medical results, consider their academic progress, and make assumptions about their needs. But I will never be able to know what life looks like through their eyes, or sounds like in their ears, or feels like in their bodies. I'll never be able to read their minds, or see the inter-connected structures of their brains, or know how their individual wiring makes them who they are. I will never know how each expe-rience in their lives, positive and negative (there are no neutral events) have shaped them into who they are. Only they themselves will know. Parenting would be much simpler if I could be within them and experience life as they experience it. Of course, it is not possible to live as your child, thus we have to rely upon their expert-ise. Every child, regardless of age or capacity, is their own expert. They know themselves.

As I raise my children, however, I do need to rely upon my expertise and the knowledge of doctors, therapists, and teachers. When my children were young, I had to be the expert and had to rely upon the expertise of other professionals. I had to listen to the spoken, and more important, the unspoken, and then I had to try my best to meet their needs. As my children grew, it became apparent that although I did my best, I wasn't always correct. As they got older (younger than you would expect, maybe preschool), they were able to express their own needs and help me help them. My children were able to explain how it looked and felt to be them. Children know themselves best and can tell us how best to help them achieve their fullest potential.

Blue Paper
Marco, adopted in 2007 at 10 months of age

I talked and talked and talked to your classroom teachers and reading teachers for four years and no one listened. They would dismiss my concerns regarding your struggles with reading and writing. They considered you to be learning and progressing right on the edge of normal, but normal enough for them. But not normal for you; I knew you had tremendous potential. You and I were told that if you only tried a little harder, applied yourself, and attended to the lessons, you could achieve. You knew you were falling behind your classmates and used humor to get through the school day. You were feeling defeated and had convinced yourself that you were stupid (which you are not!).

After many different specialists and lots of tests, finally an answer! You have very serious vision problems. Although your visual acuity is a perfect 20/20, you have muscular and neurological challenges that have made learning to read and write nearly impossible. Your eyes don't work well together, which causes issues with depth perception and figure/ground distinction. Your eyes don't adjust quickly between looking far and looking near, so when you looked at the white board and then down to your work on your desk or vice versa the words and numbers were blurry. Your eye muscles were sluggish and thus your eyes tired easily and were very sensitive to light. Your peripheral vision was seriously limited; one teacher equated it to looking through a paper towel roll. You could only see a small part of the white board and only a couple of words at a time in your book. No wonder you were not paying attention in class, learning how to read and write, or mastering math and science lessons. It was the very end of your second grade school year that we finally had some answers. We were anxious for the new school year to start.

Boy, did we luck out! Your third-grade teacher was amazing and your reading teacher was exceptional! Your classroom teacher had been teaching for more than twenty years and was considered the best third-grade teacher in the school district. I had to agree. Your reading teacher was also an experienced teacher; but even more important, she had two children who had similar vision problems and she knew how to help you. They were the first educators to really listen to me, and more important, to you. I met with your classroom teacher and your reading teacher to explain your vision challenges and discuss possible strategies to help you. We all agreed that you would know best how to accommodate your vision needs, so your classroom teacher and reading teacher met with you. You told your classroom teacher that you needed "eye breaks" when your eyes got tired, and you both agreed that when your eyes hurt, you would put your head down or cover your head with your hoody. You explained that you could only see a little bit of the white board, but could see all the work on a computer screen. So when your teacher used the white board you would sit at her desk and use her computer screen instead of looking at the white board. You also told your teachers that the black print on white paper hurt your eyes. Your reading teacher asked if colored paper or colored filters laid over your work would help. You agreed to try. Your classroom teacher took you to the paper closet and you picked out the color green; she copied all of your work onto green paper. You tried that color for a couple of months, but then asked if you could try a different color. You went back to the paper closet and chose blue; that worked like a charm. Your reading teacher ordered yellow-, green-, and blue-tinted overlays to use when you read books or used the computer screen. What a difference blue paper made in your ability to see your work. It was miraculous. You still use blue paper for all of your school work. With the instructional modifications and classroom accommodations that you requested, you progressed more in one school year than you had in total during all three years previously. You started the school year reading at a first grade level and ended the year reading at grade level. Your writing skills improved and you were starting to understand math. You knew what you needed to be successful.

You started fourth grade with great hope and excitement. You liked your new teacher and classmates. Your vision had regressed over the summer, but we were working hard to recover with vision therapy at home. Your fourth-grade teacher, new reading teacher, and I spoke about your challenges and the strategies that worked well last year. They listened; at least, I thought they did. I asked them to meet with you, explaining that you were the expert and could help them help you. These meetings never occurred. You became frustrated and angry. You were struggling with the work and were certain that you would never pass fourth grade. I went to the school's open house and upon walking into your fourth-grade classroom, I was overwhelmed by the visual stimuli. Every inch of the four walls and window shades was covered with brightly colored and cluttered posters, student artwork, signs, instructional cues, motivational sayings, and listing of homework assignments. My eyes were exhausted after a few minutes; I could not imagine being you in that classroom.

Luckily, I had an opportunity to transfer you to another elementary school within the school district. I was worried about moving you part way into the school year, but I knew that your needs would not be met in your current setting. So in October, you moved to the classrooms of two fourth-grade teachers who shared the course load; one teaching math and science and the other teaching language arts and social studies. Both of these teachers knew of our family because they had taught your older sisters. Within a week of arriving at your new school, we had a meeting to explore your unique visual needs and to develop strategies to accommodate your differences. Your teachers, the school psychologist, and I, and most important, you, attended the meeting. You were only nine years old, and there you were, voicing your needs and telling the adults how to best help you. I explained the visual challenges and you told the teachers what the classroom looked like to you. You told them that the words on the page move, that you don't see spaces between the words you write, that you only see a portion of the white board, that things look blurry when you look from the white board down to the work on your desk, that white paper hurts your eyes, and that your eyes get tired and hurt throughout the school day. They listened and heard you; they got it. The teachers asked how to help you and you were able to tell them what works for you: computer screen versus white board, eye breaks, and blue paper. Both of these teachers were very responsive to your needs and checked in with you regularly to make sure that the accommodations they were using were still helping you and to ask you if there were other strategies you would like to try. After about a month in your new school, you came home and happily announced, "I know I can pass fourth grade now!"

The Karate Kids
Wu LeBin, adopted in 2015 at almost 8 years of age

I came to China prepared for you to play with your new sisters and brother. I brought toys that you could play with independently, two of the same toy for you to parallel play with a new sibling, puzzles that required interaction but not cooperation, and games that required turn-taking with your new brother or with your sisters. I brought toys and games that were designed to help develop attachments with your new family. It was all very well thought out. I thought I was prepared for anything. Turns out I was totally unprepared for you.

You did like one of the games that I brought (a gift from a friend): *Let's Go Fishing*. You had to use a small fishing pole to catch fish that opened and closed their mouths as they rotated around a plastic pond. At first, you gave your sisters and brother a fishing pole and I was hopeful that you could all play together. However, you pointed to your sister to try to catch a fish, but then quickly gathered the fishing poles and played by yourself. You would watch the fish go around and around for hours. It was a very loud game and it drove us all crazy, but you loved it. You tried to figure out how their mouths opened and closed. You repeatedly organized the fish by color: a pile of orange, a pile of red, a pile of blue, and a pile of green. Then you arranged the fish by color in the plastic pond. If your sister or I moved a colored fish out of place, you stomped your feet, grunted, and returned the fish to its rightful colored area. You never actually played the game. As a matter of fact, you didn't play with any of my well-planned toys or games; or at least, you didn't play with them as they were intended.

I was at a loss for how to engage an autistic child. I did not know and neither did your siblings. It was heartbreaking to watch your brother and sisters try to play with you only to be ignored, pushed away, or worse, be the target of one of your tantrums (crying, stomping, and screaming). None of us knew what to do. Then one night while we were still in China, you watched a Chinese cartoon that was similar to *Power Rangers* (that you now love!) with lots of action and Kung Fu fighting. You then walked over to your sister and started karate chopping, kicking, and saying "hi-yah." You and your sister karate-chopped each other, then your brother joined in and soon your older sister decided to get into the fun. Finally, interactive play! At last, your sisters and brother could have a way to connect with you. Thank goodness the hotel room was large with lots of space for you kids to play in. Not a word was said; you just played karate. You were very serious, but your siblings were smiling and giggling. The four of you played for more than thirty minutes before you became tired. It was the first time you had really interacted with your brother and sisters; it was fun! I couldn't figure out how to get you and your siblings to play and bond with each other, but you knew how to reach out to your new siblings. You and your brother and sisters still play karate almost every day; it is still the primary way you can interact with them.

As parents, we want to be all knowing, to be the experts on our children. What I have learned is that I know my children, but I will never be all-knowing or an expert. Only they can know themselves. I've learned to respect their self-knowledge and rely upon their expertise. I've tried to empower them to advocate for themselves. I encourage them to explore their talents and interests and allow them to direct their own learning. I've learned from the experts: my children.

Birth Families Are Forever

LESSON TWELVE

Every adopted/foster child has two sets of parents: birth parents and adoptive/foster parents. It is often said that birth parents give the child life and the adoptive parents give the child a life. This is true, but simplistic. Regardless of your personal beliefs around nature versus nurture, your child's genetics, prenatal environment, and birth history sets the framework for who your child is and will become. These factors influence, shape, and effect your child throughout their lifetime. The color of their eyes, their predisposition to diseases, their personality traits, their body type and size, their vision, their learning capabilities, their physical abilities, etc., are in part determined by the genetic make-up of your child. In addition, your child's attributes, aptitudes, and challenges are affected by their experience in their birth mother's womb. Were they nourished properly? Were they exposed to alcohol or drugs in utero? Were they exposed to environmental toxins? Were they growing in a sea of stress hormones? Your child is also affected by their birth history. Were they born early? Were they deprived of oxygen during birth? Were they withdrawing from drugs? Were they born with an infection? This genetic heritage, prenatal environment, and birth history is the foundation for who our children will become. For many of our children, we don't know their genetic legacy, prenatal experience, or birth status, which can challenge us as parents; at the same time, it also frees us and our child from expectations.

Most children who enter foster care or who are adopted do not join their families at birth. Your child may come into your family after being abandoned by their birth parents and cared for in a foreign orphanage or after being abused or neglected in their birth family for months or even years. Your child's history of institutional care, abuse, and neglect also shapes who they are. It influences their personality, their cognition, their physical growth and development, their language acquisition, their social skills, their brain development, their behavior, and their capacity to build caring and positive relationships. Our children come to us with genetic and experiential histories that affect their overall person, and that history drives how we parent.

Our children's birth families also shape the lives of our children as they yearn to understand themselves and as they search for a self-satisfying self-image. Our children wonder about and search to know their birth parents to help them complete the image of themselves. They wonder who they look like and if they share any traits, talents, or quirks with their birth parents. They are thinking of their birth parents. They wish to understand their birth family or their envisioned birth family. They think about their birth heritage and culture, their racial composition, and their genetic ancestry, and try to reconcile their current identity with that of their birth family. Their birth parents shape their self-image and identity.

Your child's birth family is ever-present in your family. They are forever a part of your child and family.

Heart Surgery Needed
Rose, adopted in 2001 at 11 months of age

You were four years old when you asked me, "Did I grow in your tummy, Mommy?" I told you that you grew in your birth mother's tummy. You asked me where she lived; I told you I wasn't sure, but probably somewhere in the south of China. You told me that your Chinese mother, grandfather, and brother were shot by some bad people and they were dead. I said that that was very sad. You shook your head, but did not want to talk about it further. I told you that although you didn't grow in my tummy, that you grew in my heart. You looked at me curiously and asked in a very serious tone, "How did the doctors get me out of your heart?"

The Thumb Print
Marco, adopted in 2007 at 10 months of age

Your birth mother was young, only nineteen years old. She was not married and had given birth to a daughter a year before you arrived. I don't know if she is parenting your half-sister or if she placed her for adoption, too. She was living in a house owned by her boss. She worked as a household domestic servant and made about 600 quetzal ($80 US dollars) a month. She was not able to read or write. She had to sign the adoption paperwork with a right-hand thumb print. She told the social worker in Guatemala that she was willing to "give you up for adoption," as she did not have the financial means to care for you. It must have been a very difficult decision for your birth mother. But she put your needs first! I think of your birth mother often. Is she still a house maid? Did she have any more children? Did she marry? Has she learned to read? Is she happy? Does she wonder about you?

I wish we knew more about your birth mother and the story of your early life. We do have a picture of your birth mother holding you as a tiny baby. She is a beautiful woman with black hair, large brown eyes, and a square face. You look just like her. I'm curious to know about your birth mother's health. Is she diabetic? Your doctor is worried that you may be predisposed to the disease. Is she not able to read because of visual processing problems like the ones you are overcoming? You were only five pounds at one month of age (the first recorded weight for you). Were you born prematurely? If so, that could explain your vision processing issues. Were you exposed to smoking, drugs, or alcohol before your birth? If so, that could explain your need to use short-term memory strategies. Children born into their families have the answers to these simple questions, but you do not. It would be most helpful to have some answers for you. When I asked you what you would like to know about your birth mother, you wanted to know if she likes potato chips because you love them!

Super Stars
Pearl, adopted in 2003 at 9 months of age

I wrote in your baby book, "Happy Birthday! You are one! I thought a lot about your birth parents today. They must be distraught not knowing if you are with a loving family. It must be very difficult for them today as they remember your birth and their difficult decision to leave you. I wish they could know what a wonderful little girl you are. I thank them for their courage in letting you go so that you could become part of our family. I am so sorry that they can't see you giggle, crawl, play, and squeal."

Now that you are older, you think often of your birth parents and wonder about who they are and why they were not able to parent you. You have imagined your birth parents as Rock Stars who did not have time for you. You have assumed that they were very poor and unable to care for you. You convinced yourself that your birth parents were secret agents who needed to protect you from bad guys and thus placed you in the courtyard to be found. Most recently, you were certain that they are professional athletes, as you are an aspiring athlete. So what is the truth? I wish I knew. At dinner last week, you told me that you want to know who your birth parents are and that you are very frustrated because you will "never know for your whole life." I wish I could give you the answers you seek.

Found Abandoned

Wu LeBin, adopted in 2015 at almost 8 years of age

Your certificate of abandonment stated (literally): "This is to certify that ... [your name, gender, and birth date] ... was found abandoned nearby Yandang Village Committee ... On the same day, he was sent to the Child Welfare Institute for nursing. Up to now, there is no evidence that can prove who are his parents or other relatives though great efforts have been made to search for them."

When you were born, the only obvious challenge you would face would be a deformed right arm and hand. Your birth parents may have also noticed an odd dimple at the bottom of your spine, but would they have known what it signified? You were abandoned as a very tiny baby, a few days old. I understand why your birth parents may have left you to be found by the police; medical, educational, and therapeutic services for a disabled child in China are very difficult to find and the expertise you would require may not be available at all. In addition, your care would be extremely expensive. Unlike in the United States where we have medical insurance and public school services, your birth parents would have been responsible to pay for your medical care, your schooling, and your needed therapies. You would need many services and a lot of medical treatment throughout your lifetime. Even if your birth parents could secure the needed services and pay for your medical care and education, they would be faced with cultural biases that would have been hard to overcome for them and for you. You would have been rejected by your family and your birth parents may have been shunned. Children with special needs were hidden, mostly in orphanages. At the time of your birth, it was not culturally acceptable to have a child with special needs in China.

Nine months after your adoption and after being evaluated by fifteen medical and developmental specialists, it is now known that you have multiple challenges. As we hopped from one specialist to the next and as the medical experts debated your diagnoses and treatments, I was asked over and over, "What do you know about his family history and his prenatal care and birth?" I wish I knew. I wish I could complete the "family history" and "prenatal and birth history" sections on the many medical summary forms that I had to fill out, rather than writing over and over again "unknown." Every doctor and developmental specialist is desperate for information that could lead to an explanation(s) of your many challenges. Are any of your disorders related to prenatal factors or birth accident? Are any of your abnormalities a result of prenatal exposure to chemicals? Are any of your medical problems inherited? Are any of your conditions a result of a genetic mutation or accident? We have many questions and so far no answers. I wish we knew. Having even one of these answers could alter the course of treatment and even potentially extend your life.

I Wish You Knew
Rose, adopted in 2001 at 11 months of age

You were about eight years old and during dinner one night, you asked about your birth parents. We talked about how hard it was to not know who they were. We wondered, "Did they look like you? Do they have fun personalities? What do they do for work? What are their hobbies? Do they have any interesting talents? What are their quirks?" I wish we knew. You, however, wished they knew you. You told me that you wanted to know your birth parents because you wanted them to know that you are happy and growing into an amazing young lady. You wanted to assure them that you are safe and loved. You were able to understand that just as you will never know your birth parents, your birth parents will never have the joy of knowing you. You appreciated that your birth parents will forever wonder if you were found and brought somewhere safe (they abandoned you at the crossing of West Street). They don't even know that you are alive and thriving. They don't know that you have a mommy, a sister and two brothers, that you are excelling in school, that you play the trumpet and piano, that you volunteer at school and in your community, that you are a good friend, and that you are silly and fun. They must also yearn to know if you look like them, if you have a personality similar to theirs, if you excel in the same school subjects as they did, if you enjoy hobbies like theirs, if your talents came from them, and if you have their quirks. Your wish was for your birth parents to know you, to gift your birth parents with peace of mind.

As I look around the dinner table each day, I see the beautiful faces of my children and the faces of their birth mothers, their birth fathers, their birth grandparents, and their many other birth ancestors. My children's genetic make-up, birth experiences, and racial and cultural histories give my children the framework upon which they build their personal identities. As their mother, I foster their development upon, and within, this base framework. I also respect their connection to their birth family and encourage my children to develop a relationship (actual or imagined) with their birth family. I give them permission to love both me and their birth parents. I thank each of my children's birth parents for blessing me with their child to raise and love.

Resiliency is Miraculous
LESSON THIRTEEN

It is truly miraculous to see a child flourish in the care of a loving family. Most foster and adopted children have histories of abusive or neglectful care whether in a birth family, previous foster home, group home, institution, or orphanage. These children are faced with unthinkable challenges as they strive to survive without a loving family. Children entering foster care are all victims of physical abuse, neglect, emotional torment, and/or sexual abuse. Children in institutional/orphanage care (in the United States and abroad) most often have inadequate nutrition, substandard medical care, unresponsive and unstimulating environments, limited educational or therapeutic resources, influential peer groups (typically negative), and too few consistent caregivers. These children arrive in their new homes with emotional scars, behavioral difficulties, and developmental challenges.

Foster and adopted children have a great capacity to recover from the effects of abuse and substandard care once in the care of a loving and nurturing family. Again and again, I have witnessed the amazingly quick development of skills within days and months of a child joining a caring family. Developmental delays usually improve rapidly after foster placement or adoption, with many children making developmental gains faster than the normal maturation curve. The emotional scars typically take longer to heal, but the children become healthier over time with support and guidance. Children are incredibly resilient.

The McDonald's Happy Meal Toy
Pearl, adopted in 2003 at 9 months of age

While in China adopting you, we were ready for a change from eating Chinese food and were longing for American food, so we went to the Hard Rock Café in Guangzhou, China for lunch. Unfortunately (or fortunately), it was closed, so we went next door to McDonald's and got you a Happy Meal. I wasn't a big fan of McDonald's food, and you were not yet eating solid food, so we gave the food to another mom who was craving French fries though we kept the toy for you. The toy was Snoopy (Charlie Brown's fun-loving dog) in a baseball uniform. You could push a button on the back of the toy and Snoopy would swing a baseball bat. You loved the toy and grabbed immediately for the bat.

A week earlier, I had been looking out over the Pearl River in Guangzhou, China, waiting to meet you. You were traveling with four other babies from a Chinese orphanage about an hour and a half away by car to the government office where I would see you for the first time. We arrived at the Civil Affairs Office at 9:00 a.m., but you and the other babies were not there yet. I had joined four other families who were filling out adoption paperwork when we heard that the babies had arrived. I could no longer concentrate on the paperwork and desperately wanted to meet you. Your nanny took you and the other babies into a playroom across the hall from us and wouldn't bring any of you to the families until all the paperwork was complete. Finally, the babies started arriving and families were being united. You were the last one to arrive from across the hall. You were so cute with your spiky hair. The government official asked me why I wanted to adopt you, and I told her that I loved you. I then promised to never abuse or abandon you. The official asked if I was "satisfied with the baby"; I, of course, said yes!

You came to me gladly without a tear or struggle. You gulped down a bottle and fell asleep. It seemed all too easy. When you awoke, we both woke up to the reality of the situation. When we got back to the hotel, I undressed you to find you wearing layers of clothes even though it was a very warm spring day. You had on yellow socks, a long sleeved t-shirt, a beautiful pink sweater, and a white jumper with animals on it. You were a chubby and healthy little girl. You turned nine months old on that day, but you didn't act like a nine-month-old baby. You were extremely developmentally delayed. You had pretty good head control, but couldn't hold your head straight for very long and often rested your chin on your chest. You were not able to roll over or sit up. It was like your belly was full of jelly. Your legs were bent up and very rigid. You were not able to lie flat or sit at a ninety-degree angle. Your legs and hips were very stiff; you were like the Tin Man needing some oil. You did not reach out for toys, nor did you localize to sound (of course, later we discovered you had ear infections). I was concerned, but knew (hoped) that with some work you would catch up developmentally. Nine-month-old children who have been raised by loving parents from birth would be rolling, crawling, sitting up, pulling up to a stand, cruising along furniture, babbling, having "baby conversations" with their parents, manipulating toys, and laughing. You could do none of that. I immediately started to exercise your arms, legs, and trunk and gave you baby massages. Within only a few days you rolled over and did not tire as quickly when holding up your head.

Two days after your adoption, we traveled to your orphanage. It was newly constructed and you had only lived there for a couple of months. Your original orphanage was in the middle of the city and had been torn down so that the city could build apartment buildings. We drove through the countryside and saw rice fields, duck farms, water buffalo, and people in the fields tilling the soil with hoes. We drove over very bumpy dirt roads to your orphanage on the outskirts of a small city. The director of the orphanage greeted us and told us about the history of the institute and explained that the orphanage housed orphaned children and elderly adults. The workers then took us to see the baby rooms. There were two rooms with cribs around the edge of each room and two rows of cribs back to back in the middle of the rooms. Your crib was the last one on the left in the middle of the room. There was a long narrow patio outside the baby rooms where babies were sitting in bouncy chairs and walkers. Only three days ago you had been sitting in this row (which may explain your flexed hips). It was very nice to visit, but it was very difficult to say good-bye and leave all the other children behind.

You developed so quickly; it is like watching development in fast forward. Your fifth day in our family proved to be your most eventful. Your aunt, who traveled with us, spent days teaching you how to blow raspberries, and on day five, you did it. You also started to reach out to bat at toys that same day. And after fifteen minutes of me exercising and manipulating your legs and hips you sat up, though only for about five seconds. The next day, you started to vocalize (you liked to talk to yourself in a mirror). You also discovered your feet and grabbed your toes. The day before we were to travel home, only ten days after your adoption, you sat in a highchair propped up by a blanket; you giggled, and grabbed for a toy. How quickly you had developed after leaving your orphanage and joining our family.

We had been home for nine days and you were adjusting well. You were developing so quickly. You could then sit up, once I put you in the position, for up to fifteen minutes. You were reaching and playing with toys. You started scooching on your belly and rocking back and forth on your hands and knees (a precursor to crawling). You enjoyed cooing and screeching. You loved to "talk" to your sister and grandparents. You giggled a lot, mostly at your big sister.

By thirty days after your adoption, you had learned how to get from a sitting position to your belly. And you crawled; you crawled for about three inches, but you did it! You preferred to move through the house on your belly; it is much quicker and easier. You could finally sit up by yourself. Just two weeks later, you were babbling up a storm. You were very curious and examined everything you could get your hands on. You liked to look at books. You worked hard to stand up by yourself, which made you grin with pride. You clapped for yourself, giggled, and then fell down. You got right back up to do it again. Your sister also clapped for you and said, "Yay."

It had been two months since you came home, and you took your first shaky steps while holding my hands. During those two months, you also grew two inches, two pounds, and two shoe sizes—wow! Only four days after your first birthday and just a few days more than three months after your adoption, you took your first step! It was truly astounding to see you flourish within the care of a loving family.

Once you were on your feet, nothing was going to stop you. After being extremely developmentally delayed prior to adoption, you were now exceeding developmental expectations. On your fourth birthday, you announced that you wanted the training wheels taken off your bike. I guided you once or twice down a small hill of grass in your grandparents' front yard. Then you took off by yourself on your bike around their driveway, grinning ear to ear. A year later, you decided to play baseball and loved playing catch with your grandfather. You played boys' baseball for eight years and earned the respect (and admiration) of your male teammates. You are now an exceptional softball player. You also play field hockey, tennis, and basketball and love all physical activity (well, maybe except for volleyball). You are now fourteen years old and are determined to continue your extraordinary transformation from a baby who, strapped into a bouncy seat at an orphanage, could not roll over or sit up at nine months of age to a talented athlete with dreams of playing college softball. As I look into your future, I can see you at softball practice, while your McDonald's toy (Snoopy swinging a bat) sits on a shelf in your college dorm room.

Back to School
Cole, fostered at 6 to 7 years of age

It was a bitterly cold night and you, your toddler sister, and your mother were found walking around the city looking for a safe place for the night. The Child Protective Services caseworker had been searching for you for hours. After multiple child abuse hotline calls about your birth family and numerous attempts to provide your family with preventative services, it was determined that you were not safe in the care of your birth mother and stepfather. The caseworker found you on the streets that night to remove you from your parents and bring you into the safety of my foster home. The caseworker took you back to your parents' apartment to grab a few stuffed toys and clothes and then brought you to my house around nine o'clock at night. You arrived a few days before Christmas and the schools were closed for the next two weeks. So you settled in.

Soon the Christmas holiday was over and it was time to return to school. You were in kindergarten, but didn't know the alphabet, could not recognize any numbers, knew only two shapes, couldn't write or recognize your name in print, and had not yet learned how to tie your shoes. You were a very bright boy, but you were significantly behind your peers. Your teacher was concerned. She told me that you had missed a lot of school, and when you came, you were unprepared to learn. You did not have any school supplies, your homework was never done, and you did not focus in the classroom. I was very surprised when your teacher told me that you had recently been diagnosed with Attention Deficient Hyperactivity Disorder (ADHD). Now that you were in my foster home, you attended school every day, and every evening you and I worked to get you caught up. By the end of the school year, not only had you caught up to your peers, you had surpassed them. You were reading, adding, writing short stories, and tying your own shoes. And you were no longer diagnosed with ADHD (an obvious misdiagnosis). You were very proud of yourself and your accomplishments, just as you should have been.

The night before your first day of first grade, you and I talked about the previous school year's struggles and triumphs. With tears in my eyes, I listened to you explain that when living with your stepfather and mother, you couldn't pay attention at school because your mind was worried about what was going to happen when you got home. Were you going to have food? Were you going to get hit, thrown, or whipped? Were you going to be screamed at and belittled? Were you going to need to protect your mother from your stepfather's violence? Were you going to have to walk the streets because it wasn't safe at home? How could anyone have been able to learn when their mind was full of that kind of worry and distress?

Children have the tremendous capacity to overcome early struggles and thrive in a family. All of my children survived abandonment, neglect, and/or abuse and arrived into my home with developmental delays, nutritional deficits, medical challenges, and emotional scars. Once in a healthy and nurturing family, children can change, adapt, and flourish. A loving family is critical to a child's resiliency.

Be Grateful
LESSON FOURTEEN

It is human nature to take for granted the people and the things we have in our lives. My children help me to rejoice in the gifts we have in our lives, from the very small things, like having indoor plumbing and every day occurrences like the kindness of others, to the most important thing in life: the lives and well-being of my family. We all need to be appreciative, thankful, and grateful.

I Have a Brother
Pearl, adopted in 2003 at 9 months of age

When you were twelve years old, we went out to dinner to celebrate Chinese New Year. Halfway through dinner, I asked you, your sister, and your brother what you thought about having another brother. I explained that I was considering adopting an older boy with special needs from China. As a soon-to-be teenager, I expected you to say no way. I figured you would say you didn't want another pesky brother or that having another child would mean we would have less time and less money for your activities. Instead, your face lit up and you said, "Yes!" Your older sister also got very excited and enthusiastically agreed. Your brother, who was eight years old at the time, appeared dazed by the question. As we talked more about what it might be like to have another child, your brother continued to be stunned. He just sat quietly and stopped eating (and your brother never stops eating), so I asked him what questions he had;

he had two. First, when he had friends come for a sleepover, would his new brother have to sleep in the same room? I assured him that his brother would not sleep with him and his friends. That got a little smile. Second, as the youngest child in the family, he was the first kid to open Christmas presents at Grandma and Grandpa's house, and he did not want that to change. I told him that he and his new brother could open their gifts together. Once I clarified those two questions, your brother couldn't wait to have a brother.

Later that night, I showed you a short video (about twenty seconds) of a little boy waiting in an orphanage in China who I was considering. I was told that he was six years old and a healthy child with an arm and hand deformity. You thought he was adorable. You and your siblings studied and studied that video to find features or mannerisms that were similar to your own. He had a beauty mark on his chin like your sister. He had a strong square face like your brother. He was a quick runner like you. You all found a way to connect to him right from the start. A couple of months later, we received a second video and again you each discovered things about him that you could relate to; he was eating chocolate pudding and you all liked pudding. So, even before you met your brother, he was your brother. Without even realizing it, we all fell in love with him.

You met your brother in a government office in China. He was already at the office when we arrived, and he was brought over to us as soon as we entered the room. I saw him and knelt down with you, your sister, and brother, all standing directly behind me. His caregiver guided him over to us and he was told to give me a hug (he put his arms around me, but it wasn't a real hug). He quickly turned his back to me and stood in front of us. He never acknowledged you or your siblings' existence. You tried to say hello, but he did not respond. It was in that less-than-one-minute interaction that I knew he was autistic.

We were in the government office with him for almost two hours taking pictures needed for adoption documents and signing guardianship papers. Your new brother was running randomly around the office and disrupting the adoption proceedings for other families. There was a room adjacent to the office with exercise equipment for the government employees. We took your brother in there and he enjoyed playing on the equipment and watching the wheels turn on the exercise bikes. You, your siblings, and your aunt watched him flit from one exercise machine to the next. He never communicated with you, or played with you regardless of your numerous attempts. I'm sure that you did not understand what I knew: your brother was autistic and would never have a typical brother-sister relationship with you. I was devastated. What had I done to my family? I wanted you to have a brother.

Over the next five days in China, you and your siblings tried to connect with your new brother. Most of your attempts ended without success. You were the most successful of all your siblings. You and your new brother found a way to play together. You played karate, and he allowed you to help him put together a car. You and your older sister figured out, after the first few days, that your new brother was not typical. I tried to explain that he was autistic, but I'm not sure you understood, or at least understood what that would mean over the lifetime of our family (I knew).

Against better judgment, your aunt and I took you all to the zoo in Guangzhou, China. It was a beautiful zoo with many animals that you had never seen before. The zoo was packed with kids, parents, and grandparents. With your new brother screaming, crying, and kicking me, we made our way through the first section of the zoo with your aunt pointing out to you all the interesting animals. To get to the next section of the zoo, we had to pass through the gift shop. To calm your brother, I purchased a toy for him. You and your siblings also bought souvenirs for yourselves. Wu LeBin picked out a truck, your sister Rose got a panda jacket, your brother Marco got a dinosaur that was a bubble-making machine, and you got a little stuffed panda bear. Just to the left of the store was a stone wall and about ten feet of empty space (no people, no animals—yeah!). So we quickly sat down to claim this area. You and your aunt went out to search for food and came back with lunch: ice cream and soda! You kids thought ice cream for lunch was so cool. With his ice cream in his hand, your new brother, Wu LeBin, was spinning and spinning in circles in the ten feet of space we had found. Your other brother, Marco, was able to temporarily stop Wu LeBin's spinning by distracting him with the bubbles coming from the dinosaur's mouth. Wu LeBin screamed with excitement as he tried to pop the bubbles. I sat, exhausted, watching Wu LeBin spin and scream, with tears streaming down my face. You glanced my way and I said, "I'm so sorry; I wanted you to have a brother." You put your hand on my shoulder and told me, "I have a brother."

The Straight Letter
Rose, adopted in 2001 at 11 months of age

After ten months of excruciating time spent waiting for you, I was expecting a referral of a baby from the China Center for Adoption Affairs within the next couple of weeks. I was getting so excited. My adoption agency called on Thursday, February 22, 2001; my heart skipped a beat when I saw the phone number come up on my phone. I answered the phone, ready to hear that I was a mom and you were my daughter. Well, that is not why they had called. The Chinese Center for Adoption Affairs had changed its rules about single women adopting from China. China was now requiring single women to prove that they are not homosexual. How was I supposed to do that? I had to write a letter assuring China that I was not gay and planned to marry a man when the right one came along. Another delay of at least three or four weeks was added onto my wait for you. I was crushed; the wait was already unbearable, and now I would have to wait even longer. My adoption process was on hold with China until they received my sexual orientation letter.

I wrote that silly letter the same day. The letter had to be signed, county certified, sealed by the New York State Secretary of State, authenticated by the Chinese Embassy and then translated. It took about a month to get this letter to the Chinese Center for Adoption Affairs. Then I started waiting again; but to my great disappointment, my referral of you was delayed! All the other families whose dossier (application to China) was received in April, 2000, got "the call" and received their referral of their children. I anxiously waited for "the call," but the call never came. Because of my "straight letter," I had not yet been matched with you. I was very disappointed, sad, angry, frustrated, devastated, and emotionally exhausted. I wrote in your journal, "My heart aches to meet you; I can't take it much longer."

My adoption agency's China facilitator, Henry, checked on the status of my "straight letter" and told me that it was accepted and that my dossier was finally in the "matching room." China was choosing the right child for my family, and that was to be you! So two months after the request for the "straight letter," I got the call; I got your referral. I was overjoyed! I was finally a mom: your mom.

Without the "straight letter" and my delay of two months, you would not have been my daughter. I would have had another child who was not meant to be mine. My delay led me to you. I am now forever thankful for China's unexpected need for confirmation of my heterosexuality. I am eternally grateful to have you as my daughter.

A Shoe Salesman
Rose, adopted in 2001 at 11 months of age

It was finally time to go home. Our plane was leaving only three hours after your U.S. visa arrived, so we had to rush. We were all packed and waiting in the lobby. The adoption facilitator handed me your passport with the U.S. visa and your immigration documents. We said our quick good-bye and then climbed into a cab that was to take us to the airport. The Guangzhou airport was bustling with people and was under construction. We were on our own. We successfully got through security, but then quickly lost our way. It was just one hour before our flight was to take off and we could not find our gate. We tried to figure out where to go, but because of the construction in the airport very few signs were up and almost all the signs were only in Chinese. We looked out of place in a sea of Asian faces and we all stood more than a foot taller than the rest (as you must know, your family is very tall). We must have looked a little frazzled and worried, which we were.

We came to the attention of a very kind Chinese man. I wish I could remember his name. He was a Chinese businessman who spoke English fluently. He worked for Payless Shoes and was traveling to the United States on business. This man approached us and asked if he could help. We were so relieved! We quickly said, "Yes, please!" We explained our situation and showed him our boarding passes. Unbelievably, he was on the same flight as us from Guangzhou to Hong Kong. He walked us to the gate and we sat together as we waited for boarding.

The gentleman politely asked about you. I explained that I had just adopted you from the Guanxi Province and we were going home to New York in the United States. He thought you were very cute. He explained that due to his country's one-child policy, many little girls are abandoned and he was glad that you now had a family. He told us that he was embarrassed by his country's inability to care for all the abandoned girls. He was sad for losing you but he was very glad that you had a family. He thought your adoption and move to the United States was what was best for you. He knew that you would have many opportunities in the United States that you would not have in China. This very gentle man told us that he was thankful to us for adopting you. I explained that we were grateful to his country for the honor of adopting you. We thanked him for his help and his kind words. We parted in Hong Kong and wished each other the best. I will always remember this man's kindness and compassion.

Although within the busyness of my family's life, I may lose sight of being thankful, I am always grateful. I am grateful for so many things. I will be forever indebted to my children's birth families for making the difficult choices that led their children to me. I am thankful for the kindness of family, friends, and strangers who have made my parenting possible. I am grateful for the unexpected, as it has often brought the greatest joy to my family. I am very glad that as I am writing these words, my boys are very loudly playing karate behind me. I am very glad for the silliness, cheers, and laughter that my children bring to our lives every day. I am appreciative of my children's self-knowledge, self-expression, and personal advocacy. I am happy that my children trust in me and that we share mutual love and respect. I am in awe of my children's care and compassion and am grateful for their teaching of these important values. I am thankful for my children's demands for me to be responsive, flexible, and creative in my parenting, and for their insistence on my persistence. I am so glad for each of my children's resiliency and ability to overcome challenges to reach their fullest potential. I will treasure the gift of forgiveness. I will always be thankful for having found my life's purpose through adoption. In the midst of our very hectic life (work, school, concerts, softball clinics, doctor appointments, school meetings, field trips, jazz band rehearsal, basketball games, etc.), I am most thankful for my children's daily reminder to be grateful for what is important.

Be Purposeful
LESSON FIFTEEN

I was working in a very satisfying career procuring grant funds for public schools. My job had security, flexibility, excellent benefits, state retirement, and a salary commensurate with my education. I was making a difference in the lives of thousands of students; my team brought in millions of dollars to improve teaching and learning. I felt purposeful. Then, I held my very ill daughter in my arms in China, uncertain of her survival. Once she recovered and she and I settled into a new life together, I knew that I had to dedicate my life to ensure that no other child would face death because they did not have parents. I couldn't parent all the abandoned, abused, or neglected children, but I could find them adoptive families. So I left behind my successful career in grant procurement to become an adoption social worker. After completing a Master of Social Work degree, I took a job with a small adoption agency, a position with no security, very few benefits, no retirement, and a salary less than half of what I had been making working for the schools. Yes, it was crazy. I remember that before I left the schools, at an end-of-year celebration, my supervisor announced that I would be leaving the organization to become an adoption social worker. I don't remember much of my farewell speech, but I do clearly remember saying that I had decided to change the world one child at a time.

One Grain of Sand

Rose, adopted in 2001 at 11 months and all of my children

I had arrived on campus and was sitting in a graduate-school class full of much younger students (I had returned to school later in life) with a new professor leading the class. We were all hopeful, idealistic social workers in training, who were ready to change the world. That morning, the professor asked us to visualize ourselves at the edge of the ocean with our feet in the waves, our bodies being rocked by the tide, and our eyes looking out over the endless horizon. The professor instructed us to visualize ourselves in relationship to the enormity of the world and its problems. She and my classmates spoke of how small they felt in relation to the power and seemingly endlessness of the ocean. The students spoke about their insignificance within the universe, the millions of people on the earth who need help, and the complexities of the world's problems. My classmates convinced themselves that they could have very little impact on the world. The students decided that the strength of the waves would knock us down and render us helpless. They were overwhelmed by the vastness of the challenges and were paralyzed by feelings of inconsequentiality and powerlessness against the forces of the world.

After you, my first daughter, nearly died in a foreign orphanage, I had found my purpose. I learned that I was powerful and my actions were consequential. I could make a difference in the world. I decided to leave my very secure and fulfilling career to dedicate my life to finding families for orphaned children around the globe. I could not bear to think that another child could lose their life simply because they didn't have parents. I needed to earn my Master of Social Work degree so that I could work in the field of adoption. So as I was approaching forty, I returned to school part time while still working full time and caring for you, a very sick baby. During my second semester, I adopted your sister from China. Three years later, I earned my degree, passed my boards (professional licensing exam), and became a Licensed Master Social Worker. I then began my career finding families for children without parents.

Many years later, after parenting you and your siblings and finding families for hundreds of orphaned children, I reflected back on my professor's visualization exercise and was able to gain a new understanding of the lesson. I believe the true message was that although each of us is but a very small part (a grain of sand) of the enormous universe, each of us is important and powerful in shaping the world; each of us has a purpose and everyone impacts on the well-being of our society. Every grain of sand affects every other grain of sand. If it were not for this one grain of sand, the sand touched by it would not be affected in the same way and those particles of sand would impact on the surrounding grains of sand in a different way and so on and so on, until every grain of sand is altered by the presence or absence of that one grain of sand. Rose, as one very important grain of sand, you have certainly changed my life and the lives of every individual you touch.

This visualization exercise also taught me that every speck of sand is acted upon and shaped by every other speck of sand and by the waves rolling across it. A person's environment alters the life of that individual. Every child and adult is shaped by the influences of the world. You have been molded by your genetic history, prenatal environment, health challenges, neurological capacities, physical abilities, early childhood experiences (e.g., abandonment, institutionalization, and neglect), adoptive family life, parenting, your extended family, friends, teachers, classmates, community culture and opportunities, societal expectations, environmental factors (e.g., pollution), global events, and so on.

Simultaneously, you are being shaped by the world and changing the world. In all the grains of sand on this earth, whether next to one another or across the sea; whether on the shores of the hurricane-prone Gulf Coast or the beaches of the Atlantic Ocean or the calm seas of China, each grain of sand shapes the world. Every individual across the globe, no matter how tiny or mighty, has an impact on the current and future world. Every individual is significant, powerful, and has the ability to change the world. You, your sister, and your brothers are important, influential, and have and will continue to transform the world.

I ask that you visualize yourself at the edge of the ocean with your feet in the waves, your body being rocked by the tide, and your eyes looking out over the endless horizon. How can you use your power as one grain of sand to change the future of the world? What is your purpose?

The Baby in the Bouncy Seat
Pearl, adopted in 2003 at 9 months of age

She was very tiny and was lying in a blue bouncy seat on the patio of the third floor of your orphanage. I would guess that she was about six months old. I knelt down with you asleep in my arms and tried my best to interact with her. At first, she averted my gaze, then she looked at me, or should I say through me. She did not smile, giggle, or make any sounds; but of course, I'm not very entertaining. The little girl sitting next to her, also tied into a blue bouncy seat with red straps, did give me a smile and reached out for my hand.

Your orphanage was in a rural community about an hour and a half from a large city. It was newly built and was at the end of a dirt road surrounded by small farms. The patio where these little ones sat overlooked a small pond and farmland. However, these girls were facing the white walls of their crib rooms rather than out over the view of the countryside. The orphanage was very clean and sterile: white walls, cement floors, and lots of windows. I did not see any books, hear any music, see any pictures or murals on the walls, or find any toys (except for one tricycle that was being ridden by an older boy with visual impairments). According to the orphanage director, they care for approximately one hundred children a year with almost seventy of these children being adopted by U.S. families each year. During our visit, there were about sixty babies under a year old (all girls), a toddler boy, a four-year-old with crossed eyes, and a young girl with Down syndrome (she gave you a kiss on the cheek) living at the orphanage.

Your caregivers brought us to the third floor of the institute and showed us your crib. There were two baby rooms housing thirty babies each with cribs around the edge of each room and two rows of cribs back to back in the middle of the rooms. Your picture and name card was on your crib. They let me take your name card for you to keep. You had a blanket, a pillow, and a crocheted purple and pink teddy bear in the crib. In the second baby room were the younger babies. Four of them were tiny babies, not more than two months old. All the babies were bundled in many layers of clothes and blankets. The youngest baby was lying in a basinet with a dark purple plaid liner and small pink pillow. She was covered with multiple layers of blankets with a red blanket on top, tucked tightly around her. All you could see was her beautiful face. One baby was crying. I spoke with her and she quieted for a minute and then started screaming again. A caregiver finally came to get her and gave her a bottle. The caregivers were very loving, but were being asked to do the impossible, to be a parent to one hundred babies.

There was a long narrow patio outside the baby rooms. There were about thirty babies lined up along the back of the patio. They were all wearing the same thing: yellow plaid pants and a red shirt, except one baby who was wearing pink pants. She was smaller than the rest and had a cleft lip. Half of the babies were sitting in blue cloth bouncy chairs and the other half were sitting in blue or pink walkers. I stopped and played with a few of the babies. One of the babies sitting in a blue walker giggled at my silliness.

I'm so glad to have seen where you lived and to have met your caregivers. It was difficult to say good-bye. You didn't fuss when it was time to leave, but I wanted to throw a hissy fit about having to leave all the other children behind. I couldn't take all the babies home with me that day, but I came to the realization that I could help find them families.

Mom, I Need
All of my children

Listen in for just a few moments to what my children have needed and communicated to me with their words, their behaviors, and their silence. Mom, I need my basketball uniform for team pictures today, can you please bring it to the school now? Mom, I need money for lunch today. Mom, eating is painful and I can't eat enough to keep me healthy; I need a feeding tube to help me grow. Mom, I can't find matching socks (I have six single socks) can you please get me some? Mom, I need you to chaperone my field trip to the zoo. Mom, I can't read, I need you to make the words stop moving across the page. Mom, I need you to sign a permission slip so that I can go to New York City with my school. Mom, I have no words, but please figure out that the tiny bone in my deformed thumb was accidently fractured on the playground and it hurts. Mom, I need to get to softball practice on time (please try). Mom, my nose itches and my lungs hurt when I run far, I need (but don't want) allergy shots for the next five years. Mom, I need some alone time; playing with my brother is overwhelming right now. Mom, I need a snack! Mom, I need to understand why my birth parents left me at the entrance of a village rather than parent me. Mom, I need a ride home; I missed the bus again. Mom, I need a white shirt and black pants for the band concert and oh yeah, it's tomorrow. Mom, I threw up at school this morning because I'm stressed out in a regular classroom; I need a small classroom and a teacher that understands my special needs. Mom, I need my bowling shoes, but I can't find them. Mom, I'm smart but can't get my homework done; I need more time to finish my work, and then I will succeed. Mom, I need a tickle fight to help me bond with you. Mom, I need new cleats and a glove for baseball. Mom, I need ….

Mom, I need you to be caring, compassionate, listening, playful, persistent, forgiving, trusting, responsive, flexible, and creative.

Mom, please embrace my birth family, be grateful for who we are and what we have, accept the unexpected, respect my self-knowledge, and remember what is important: your children.

Every individual has a reason for being, a purpose. Finding purpose in your life gives your life meaning and gives you a reason for living each day. We all search for a life purpose; fostering and adoption have given my life purpose.

Conclusion

Thank you to my children for allowing me to write their stories and for giving me the time to write them. Thank you for teaching me to expect the unexpected, and be okay with that. Thank you for encouraging me to look through your eyes, to listen to your words, actions, and silence, and trust in your self-knowledge. Thank you for teaching me how to play and giggle. Thank you for helping me to forgive and be forgiven. Thank you for allowing me to marvel in your resiliency, your caring, and your compassion. Thank you for trusting me and sharing your love. Thank you for teaching me how to parent you; for how to be responsive, flexible, and creative in my parenting of your unique challenges, strengths, and talents. Thank you for your determination and your demand for my persistence. Thank you for bringing your birth families into our family. Thank you for reminding me to be grateful for the blessings in life. Thank you for giving my life purpose. Thank you for reminding me what is important in life: my family.

Notes

[1] A squat toilet is the most common type of toilet in China. It is a toilet used by squatting rather than sitting. The toilet bowl (or pan) is at the floor level and you squat above the bowl to use the toilet.

[2] Radial dysplasia (aka radial longitudinal deficiency or radial club hand) is a rare congenital (born with it) difference in which the radius bone of the forearm did not form properly or is absent. This causes the hand to be bent inward and many children with this condition also have a missing or small nub for a thumb.

[3] Institutionalized children typically have developmental delays and may exhibit social and behavioral abnormalities because of their orphanage's deprived environment and unusual group living arrangements. Most institutional effects can be overcome. Children with "poor abilities" with organic causes have difficulties because of physical or physiological differences due to genetics, disease, or trauma. Disabilities from organic causes may or may not be treatable.

[4] Autism Spectrum Disorder (aka autistic) is a neurodevelopmental disorder that impairs a child's ability to communicate and interact with others. It also includes restricted repetitive behaviors, interests, and activities. These issues cause significant impairment in social, occupational, and other areas of functioning.

[5] Children with autism can have self-stimulatory behaviors (aka self-stim or stimming). These behaviors are repetitive or unusual body movement (e.g., rocking, spinning, hand-flapping), posturing (e.g., arching back or holding hands/fingers at an angle), visual stimulation (e.g., watching an object spin or flutter), chewing or mouthing objects, or listening to the same song or noise over and over.

[6] Spina bifida occulta is a mild form of spina bifida in which one or more vertebrae (the bones which form the backbone) fail to form properly.

[7] Attachment is the emotional connection between a child and their parent. It is a trusting relationship that is built over time. A securely attached child feels safe, protected, and loved. This attachment to a parent gives a child the security, neurological readiness, and confidence to explore his/her world.

[8] A feeding G-tube (gastrostomy tube) is a plastic tube inserted through a stoma (hole) in the abdomen into the stomach that is used to deliver nutrition (formula) directly to the stomach. It allows children with feeding problems get the fluid and calories they need to grow.

[9] Least Restrictive Environment refers to an education setting where a child with special needs can receive an appropriate education designed to meet their individual educational needs, alongside peers without disabilities to the maximum extent appropriate.

[10] A tethered spinal cord is a neurological disorder associated with spina bifida. It occurs when tissue attachments limit the movement of the spinal cord causing abnormal stretching of the spinal cord.

[11] The federal Individuals with Disabilities Education Act (IDEA) was enacted in 1975 to ensure that children with disabilities have the opportunity to receive a free appropriate public education, just like typical children. At the local school district level, the Committee on Special Education (a team of educators, therapists, and parents) is responsible for developing recommendations for special education programs and services for children with disabilities. Upon parent, physician, educator, or therapist referral, the local school district is responsible to conduct a comprehensive evaluation to determine a child's eligibility for special education services. The evaluation may consist of an analysis of a child's cognitive,

motor, language, adaptive (self-help), vision, hearing, and social/emotional skills. A school district has 60 days to complete this evaluation.